THE
DÜNGEONMEISTER
COOKBOOK

THE DÜNGEONMEISTER COOKBOOK

75 RPG-INSPIRED RECIPES TO LEVEL UP YOUR GAME NIGHT

 JEF ALDRICH & JON TAYLOR

ADAMS MEDIA

NEW YORK LONDON TORONTO SYDNEY NEW DELHI

Adams Media
An Imprint of Simon & Schuster, Inc.
100 Technology Center Drive
Stoughton, Massachusetts 02072

First Adams Media hardcover edition
April 2022

ADAMS MEDIA and colophon are trademarks
of Simon & Schuster.

For information about special discounts for
bulk purchases, please contact Simon &
Schuster Special Sales at 1-866-506-1949
or business@simonandschuster.com.

The Simon & Schuster Speakers Bureau can
bring authors to your live event. For more
information or to book an event contact
the Simon & Schuster Speakers Bureau
at 1-866-248-3049 or visit our website at
www.simonspeakers.com.

Interior design by Julia Jacintho
Interior photographs by Harper Point
Photography
Photography chefs: Chase Elder, Christine
Tarango, Alexis Plank
Interior illustrations by Daniel Govar
Interior images © 123RF/Denis Barbulat,
svitden, iloveotto

Manufactured in the United States of America

5 2023

Library of Congress Cataloging-in-Publication
Data
Names: Aldrich, Jef, author. | Taylor, Jon,
1982– author.
Title: The düngeonmeister cookbook / Jef
Aldrich & Jon Taylor.
Description: Stoughton, Massachusetts: Adams
Media, 2022. | Series: The ultimate rpg guide
series | Includes index.
Identifiers: LCCN 2021050225 |
ISBN 9781507218112 (hc) |
ISBN 9781507218129 (ebook)
Subjects: LCSH: Cooking. |
LCGFT: Cookbooks.
Classification: LCC TX715 .A3583 2022 |
DDC 641.5--dc23/eng/20211027
LC record available at
https://lccn.loc.gov/2021050225

ISBN 978-1-5072-1811-2
ISBN 978-1-5072-1812-9 (ebook)

Always follow safety and commonsense cooking
protocols while using kitchen utensils, operating
ovens and stoves, and handling uncooked food.
If children are assisting in the preparation of
any recipe, they should always be supervised by
an adult.

Dedication

To our moms, who would
like you to know the chocolate cookie
dough can be shaped into poops
and hidden around the house
for the delight of the chef.

Contents

Introduction

"You turn the corner of the tunnel and find yourself face-to-face
with a gigantic purple worm!"
"I reach for my sword!"
"I ready my bow!"
"I...wait, where's the snacks and soda?"

If there's one thing we love, it's getting together over a few board games,
a couple handfuls of dice, and a cocktail or two and making a memorable night
with good friends. One thing the whole experience has always lacked, however: great food. So, naturally, being problem solvers, experienced in dealing
with anything from gelatinous cubes to fire imps, we set out to fix this difficulty. The result...

Welcome to *The Düngeonmeister Cookbook*, a recipe guide for the game night
planner in every one of you. We've compiled a collection of seventy-five easy
recipes ready for game night sharing, focusing on finger foods, tear-and-share
delights, and scrumptious desserts that you can make at home in advance and
have ready to wow your guests and make your session special. You and your
companions will be able to nosh on such delicious fare as:

- Critical Dip: Peach Lime Salsa
- Second Breakfast: Baked Brie with Fruit Compote
- Barbarian Greatclub: Bacon-Wrapped Smoky Turkey Leg
- Philter of Love: Strawberry Buttermilk Snowballs

A little rusty or even new to cooking? Or maybe you're a seasoned cook
looking for new ideas. No problem: We've curated this collection to include
both simple and more complex recipes, from food anyone can make, like some
Genasi's Bliss (spiced peanuts), all the way to the harder stuff, like Dwarven
Battle Pasta. The easy step-by-step processes in this book will have you
proofing dough and icing cookies like a pro in no time.

So no matter your character's species or the needs of your gaming party, you'll find recipes that will suit your needs, ranging from scrumptious brunch tacos to candy snacks, fiery chicken wings, pork tenderloin, and chocolate pretzels.

There's definitely something for everyone, all organized by theme so that your game night can feature dishes that put a spotlight on your games. Taking on a dragon? Serve some Dragon Talons! Raiding a warren of kobold marauders? A bowl of Kobold Bay Scorpion Sauce will bring that extra zing to make your game come alive (even if the kobolds kill the wizard). Exploring a map? We've got a literal cookie map.

So don't settle for takeout anymore. After all, you wouldn't want to fight an undersized goblin with a bad case of the shakes, would you? (Well, maybe you would, but a lot of adventurers prefer something a bit more testing.) Treat your noshes like you would a game. Read the rules, prep for your session, and be in it to win it (and have some fun along the way). Before you know it, you'll be the talk of your tabletop. So come along with us. Grab your weapons (spatulas and whisks, we suppose), gird your loins with an apron, and get started! It's time to cook your way to a critical success at partying.

Chapter 1

DEMI-HUMAN DELIGHTS: SNACKS FOR THOSE WHO WALK UPRIGHT

We briefly considered a Human Food chapter but ultimately set that idea aside, seeing as how it's been covered by 99.9 percent of every other recipe book ever made (we're allowing for the occasional guide to pet food cookery). Instead, here you'll find a list of recipes designed to please, tantalize, and satiate various sapient species that exist only in myth and magical tome. A dangerous strategy, but sometimes you have to build the product and let it create the audience, you know? Food fit for elves, tieflings, and even kobolds (we're stepping them up to the big leagues) that you're also welcome to try if you want.

ELVEN PERFECTION:
Fig Mascarpone Tart with Honey...16

TIEFLING'S FOOD CAKE:
Spicy Devil's Food Cupcakes...19

DRAGONBORN BREATH:
Skordalia...21

KOBOLD BAY SCORPION SAUCE:
Old Bay Crab Dip...22

GOBLINTZES:
Savory Blintzes...24

GNOMISH BURROWS:
Grown-Up Dirt Cup...27

GENASI'S BLISS:
Spiced Peanuts...29

SECOND BREAKFAST:
Baked Brie with Fruit Compote...30

DWARVEN BATTLE PASTA:
Toasted Ravioli...33

ELVEN PERFECTION
Fig Mascarpone Tart with Honey

Prep Time: 4 hours, 30 minutes | Cook Time: N/A | Serves 6

Imagine a picturesque elven village nestled in the deep of the woods. Graceful, swooping architecture in harmony with the surrounding nature, open balconies and terraces that wind around the trees into the sky, and furniture crafted with grace and care. What's on the dinner table in your mind? A greasy sack of cheesesteaks? Okay, fine, yes, those are universal, but what's for dessert? What better than this delectable tart of delicate mascarpone cheese, paired with the sweetness of forest honey and sliced fig? Save the lembas bread; serve this, and you'll earn your way to the Grey Havens and thence to the Undying Lands in the West.

For Crust
⅓ cup packed light brown sugar
2 cups graham cracker crumbs
¾ teaspoon salt
7 tablespoons melted unsalted butter

For Filling
1 (8-ounce) package room-temperature
   mascarpone cheese
3 tablespoons packed light brown sugar
3 tablespoons honey
1⅓ cups heavy whipping cream, divided
2 cups fresh figs, halved
¼ cup chopped toasted pistachios
   (optional)
2 tablespoons amber honey
   (optional)

1. To make Crust: In a medium bowl, whisk together brown sugar, cracker crumbs, and salt. Add butter and stir until well combined.

2. Press mixture into the bottom and sides of a 9" springform tart pan. Place in the refrigerator to chill while preparing Filling, about 30 minutes.

3. To make Filling: In a large bowl, use an electric mixer to beat mascarpone on medium speed until creamed and no lumps remain, about 1 minute. Add brown sugar and beat to combine, about 30 seconds. With the mixer on low speed, slowly drizzle in honey. Scrape down sides of bowl and beat an additional 30 seconds.

4. In a separate medium bowl, beat 1 cup cream on medium-low speed until frothy. Continue beating at increasing speed until stiff peaks form.

5. Fold half of beaten cream into mascarpone mixture. Once combined, fold in remaining half. If the mixture remains clumpy, add additional ⅓ cup heavy whipping cream and briefly beat until smooth.

6. Spread mixture into prepared Crust and refrigerate to firm up at least 4 hours, up to three days. When ready to serve, garnish with figs, pistachios, and an extra drizzle of honey, if desired.

WHAT ABOUT ALL THE SUBRACES?

Yes, elves come in a dizzying variety of forms and styles. Wood elves with their wild green hair and feral dispositions, dark elves from the bowels of the underworld below, aquatic elves from the deep reaches of the sea, and each has a favorite tart (well, aquatic elves might not; they get soggy). To re-create these, a simple substitution is all you require! Strawberries, blueberries, peaches, and our personal favorite, kiwi, all make incredible tarts that will see your friends (and your blades) singing.

TIEFLING'S FOOD CAKE
Spicy Devil's Food Cupcakes

Prep Time: 1 hour | Cook Time: 22 minutes | Serves 24

Rich, complicated, and just a bit fiery, these cupcakes capture the devilish elements of the only-slightly-demonic folk with ease. Should you wish to take a walk on the dark side of confectionery, you can't go wrong with this sinfully chocolaty treat, though you should eat them in close company, as they will draw glares and mistrust from every street passerby.

For Cupcakes

1 (15.25-ounce) box devil's food chocolate cake mix
1½ teaspoons ground ancho chili pepper
¼ teaspoon cayenne pepper
1¼ cups water
⅓ cup vegetable oil
3 large eggs

For Frosting

1 teaspoon ground ancho chili pepper
⅛ teaspoon cayenne pepper
½ teaspoon ground cinnamon
4 cups confectioners' sugar
1 (8-ounce) package softened cream cheese
½ cup softened unsalted butter
½ teaspoon vanilla extract
48 small dried red chilies

1. To make Cupcakes: Preheat oven to 350°F. Line a twenty-four-cup muffin tin with paper liners.

2. In a large bowl, combine cake mix, ancho chili, and cayenne.

3. Using an electric mixer set to medium speed, beat in water, oil, and eggs, about 2 minutes.

4. Spoon batter evenly into muffin tin cups, filling each liner to ⅔ full.

5. Place cupcakes in oven and bake 18–22 minutes until a toothpick inserted in the center comes out clean. Remove from oven and cool completely, about 1 hour, before frosting.

6. To make Frosting: In a large bowl, combine ancho chili, cayenne, cinnamon, and sugar. Using an electric mixer, beat in cream cheese and butter on medium speed until frosting is smooth and lump-free. Mix in vanilla.

continued on next page

7. Spread frosting onto cooled cupcakes, then garnish each cupcake with 2 dried chilies stem-side up (stuck into each cupcake to create horns). Serve immediately.

INFERNALLY REGARDED

Despite all appearances and superstitions, there's nothing explicitly evil about tieflings or their namesake cakes. Sure, they're eternally cursed, linked to hellfire and darkness, and unexpectedly spicy, but that's not enough to foment suspicion. Foie gras is generally more evil if you're looking for something actually malicious, but we recommend the cupcakes. Add red food coloring to the frosting if you're feeling extra devilish.

DRAGONBORN BREATH
Skordalia

Prep Time: 30 minutes | Cook Time: 20 minutes | Serves 6

Descended from ancient lineages of dragonkind, the dragonborn are a proud race of noble, scaled adventurers and explorers, possessed of heavily muscled tails, powerful draconic features, and breath so deadly they can use it as a weapon. One small side effect of having such power in their throats is that it takes a big punch of flavor before a dragonborn starts to notice it. This potato spread, infused with enough garlic to rattle lesser creatures, is a personal favorite of theirs.

2 tablespoons salt
4 large russet potatoes, peeled
12 cloves garlic, peeled and minced
⅓ cup olive oil

3 tablespoons lemon juice
2 tablespoons chopped green onion
2 tablespoons chopped fresh parsley
1 loaf crusty French bread, sliced

1. In a large pot of water, add salt and bring to a boil over high heat. Add potatoes and cook at a boil until tender, approximately 15–20 minutes. Drain water, reserving 1 cup.

2. Use a fork or potato masher to mash potatoes in pot until smooth. Add garlic, oil, and lemon juice. Use a hand mixer or stick blender to combine all ingredients until fully smooth. If the mixture is still lumpy, add a small amount of reserved water and continue to blend.

3. Refrigerate 30 minutes and serve topped with green onion and parsley alongside bread for spreading.

APPEARANCES CAN BE DELICIOUSLY DECEIVING
Dragonborn Breath looks exactly like mashed potatoes, but don't be fooled: It's infused with far more garlic than even the most allium-heavy of side dishes. Eating this powerful concoction will see you exclaim about the explosive garlic...forcefully. Maybe don't talk right at anyone for a few minutes.

KOBOLD BAY SCORPION SAUCE
Old Bay Crab Dip

Prep Time: 10 minutes | Cook Time: 30 minutes | Serves 6

Tricky, crafty, and skittish, kobolds use the world around them in inventive ways to survive and defend themselves from outsiders, favoring tools that larger races would eschew. Whether they're using scorpions to line pit traps or just tying them to sticks, kobolds are inextricably linked with scorpions in matters of defense. It's a bonus then that kobolds find the venomous arthropods so delicious. For this party-friendly dip, we've omitted the scorpion, which is hard to source and too important to the kobold life cycle to disturb, and replaced it with a somewhat more palatable arthropod. Serve with crusty bread (baguettes or focaccia), carrots, and/or celery for dipping.

1 (8-ounce) package softened cream cheese
1 cup mayonnaise
2 teaspoons Old Bay seasoning
½ teaspoon dry mustard
1 tablespoon chopped fresh dill
 (or 1 teaspoon dried dill)
1 pound lump crabmeat
¼ cup shredded Cheddar cheese

1. Preheat oven to 350°F.

2. In a medium bowl, mix together cream cheese, mayonnaise, Old Bay, mustard, and dill. Add crabmeat and toss until just combined.

3. Spread mixture in a shallow, ungreased 1½-quart baking dish. Sprinkle with Cheddar.

4. Bake 30 minutes or until hot and bubbly. Remove from oven and serve.

DESCENDED FROM DRAGONS

Although it's never been proven, kobolds like to think they're the inheritors and children of far more fearsome dragonkind. As such, they'll often one-up each other in pursuit of the ultimate expression of draconic heritage: dragon breath. To incorporate this feature, feel free to add ½ teaspoon of cayenne pepper while blending the other ingredients, and sprinkle an additional pinch over the blend with the cheese. This will provide a mild spice, more than enough for the tiny palates of kobolds, while not overpowering the delicate flavor of the scorp...uhhh, crab.

GOBLINTZES
Savory Blintzes

Prep Time: 4 hours, 30 minutes | Cook Time: 17 minutes | Serves 8

What do goblins eat when they can't acquire man-flesh? Well, all sorts of things, really. The culinary arts may not be held in the highest regard in the warrens and camps of these little green marauders, but occasionally a great goblin chef will rise up, leading the warband on its stomach, and elevating the palates of his followers with a dish like this one—a zesty and satisfying savory blintz stuffed with cheeses, eggs, and, of course, enough greens to remind you where it came from.

5 large eggs, divided

¾ cup all-purpose flour

¾ cup whole milk

3 tablespoons melted unsalted butter

½ teaspoon plus ⅛ teaspoon kosher salt, divided

3½ tablespoons cold salted butter, divided

8 ounces frozen cut spinach, thawed and drained

½ teaspoon ground black pepper, divided

1 cup shredded fontina cheese

¾ cup whole-milk ricotta cheese

½ cup shredded Parmesan cheese

1 tablespoon finely chopped fresh thyme leaves, plus 1 tablespoon whole leaves, divided

½ teaspoon lemon zest

8 ounces sour cream

1. In a medium bowl, blend 3 eggs, flour, milk, melted butter, and ½ teaspoon salt. Cover and refrigerate 15–30 minutes until cold.

2. In a large nonstick frying pan, melt ½ tablespoon cold butter over medium-high heat. Add spinach, season with ¼ teaspoon pepper and remaining ⅛ teaspoon salt, and cook until spinach is tender, about 3 minutes. Transfer to a medium bowl and wipe pan clean.

3. In a separate medium bowl, whisk remaining 2 eggs, then stir in cheeses, chopped thyme, remaining ¼ teaspoon pepper, lemon zest, and cooked spinach. Set aside.

4. In the same frying pan used for spinach, melt ¼ tablespoon cold butter over medium-low heat. When butter is melted and spread out, add a scant ¼ cup batter and rotate and tilt pan to cover bottom. Cook until

almost set, about 30 seconds. Flip crepe and cook until it lifts away from pan edges, about 30 seconds. Transfer to a large plate and repeat seven more times with remaining batter, adding ¼ tablespoon cold butter to pan and melting before adding each additional ¼ cup batter. Stack crepes on plate and keep covered with a clean towel while cooking remaining crepes.

5. Spoon roughly 2½ tablespoons cheese filling along one-third of top crepe. Fold crepe to seal, being sure to tuck in sides. Set aside, seam-side down, and repeat filling and folding with remaining crepes.

6. Melt ½ tablespoon cold butter in pan over medium heat. Cook blintzes four at a time until just browned on both sides, about 2–3 minutes per side. Wipe pan clean and add more cold butter and melt before repeating with remaining four blintzes.

7. Top each blintz with 1 ounce sour cream and sprinkle whole fresh thyme leaves over top. Serve hot.

HOBGOBLINTZES?

Sure thing, just substitute mozzarella for the fontina cheese, replace the thyme with ¼ cup of sun-dried tomatoes (hobgoblins tend toward reddish orange instead of green, after all), and two tablespoons of minced green onions, and serve them about 50 percent more militantly. You know, salute when they hit the table, declare yourself the eternal victor of dinner, that sort of thing.

GNOMISH BURROWS
Grown-Up Dirt Cup

Prep Time: 1 hour, 20 minutes | Cook Time: N/A | Serves 5

Gnomes have come a long way since their early era (when their main defining feature was explosions). Modern gnomes build dazzling societies themed around their unique magical abilities of illusion, dancing lights, and animal communication to fill their streets with wonder and light. (And occasional explosions.) Their roots, however, are actually roots! Gnomes have always possessed a strong connection to the deep places of the earth, able to communicate with the creatures they find there. Their food still reflects their love of this subterranean world they started in, albeit usually with some modern refinements. This recipe, literally for a cup of "dirt" and "worms," however, does not feature such refinements. This is the raw gnome stuff.

16 Oreos or other chocolate sandwich cookies, crushed and divided
1 cup cold espresso
1½ ounces whiskey
1 (3.9-ounce) package instant chocolate pudding

2 cups cold whole milk
8 ounces Cool Whip or other frozen whipped topping, thawed
15 gummy worms

1. In a small bowl, combine half of crushed cookies with espresso and whiskey. Set aside to soak.

2. In a medium bowl, stir together pudding mix and milk until no lumps remain. Set aside for 5 minutes to allow mixture to firm up.

3. Stir soaked cookie mixture into pudding, along with whipped topping. Spoon mixture into 6-ounce cups or ramekins. Sprinkle each cup with remaining crushed cookies. Place 3 gummy worms over crumbled cookie "dirt" on each cup.

4. Refrigerate cups 1 hour before serving.

continued on next page

GNOMISH TINKERING

Gnomes are universally known (we won't go as far as saying "regarded") for their inventive nature and tendency to tinker up new gizmos and gadgets that explode as often as they work. Their food is similarly prone to experimentation on a level other folk may sniff at. The Dirt Cup is no exception. It's a bowl of chocolate dessert and booze. It's easy to modify. Toss in your favorites! Sprinkles, nuts, banana slices, and more will only bring positive change to this dish. And if you want to think like a gnome, toss in something unexpected!

GENASI'S BLISS
Spiced Peanuts

Prep Time: 5 minutes | Cook Time: 25 minutes | Serves 12

Bolstered by the elements that make up some portion of their heritage, the Genasi are closer to four unique species than one. The impulsive and hotheaded Fire Genasi; the stolid and dependable Earth; the mercurial and breezy Air; and the flexible, fluid Water. They do have a few things in common, of course. Their appearance always features some elements of their...element, and they share a love for the spicy, earthy, airy mixed nuts featured here. Share a bowl of these with your gathering and let the primal party commence!

3 cups salted and shelled peanuts
2 tablespoons vegetable oil
2 tablespoons granulated sugar

1½ teaspoons ground cumin
½ teaspoon cayenne pepper
½ teaspoon garlic powder

1. Preheat oven to 300°F.

2. In a medium bowl, combine peanuts and oil.

3. In a small bowl, combine sugar, cumin, cayenne, and garlic powder. Sprinkle mixture over peanuts and stir to coat completely.

4. Pour spiced peanuts onto an ungreased rimmed baking sheet, and bake 20–25 minutes until lightly browned, stirring once halfway through cooking.

5. Remove from oven and transfer to a plate to cool completely before serving, about 10 minutes.

ELEMENTARY COMPLEMENTS

Nature is eternally in balance as the four elements stand in equal opposition to one another. Fire keeps water in check as air holds against the earth. Similarly, these peanuts need some manner of complement to cleanse the palate, or they'll overtake...we don't know, the entire planet or something. As such, they work well as part of a tray of meats and cheeses. Sharp Cheddar, a little Brie, some crackers, and salami, and this dish will be eternally balanced as well. Well, balanced for about 20 minutes before they're devoured, anyway.

SECOND BREAKFAST
Baked Brie with Fruit Compote

Prep Time: 15 minutes | Cook Time: 25 minutes | Serves 6

Halflings enjoy a great many homey things, from the joys of the hearth to a simple ale, and the thing they enjoy most of all is good food served often. The Second Breakfast is perfect for this, and this dish is remarkably beautiful and suitably breathtaking when placed at the table, yet it is incredibly easy to prepare. Rich, gooey Brie baked, then piled high with a bracing herb-infused fruit compote. It's not just for elevenses anymore. Serve with crusty bread slices, crackers, grapes, strawberries, and/or nuts for topping.

For Compote
3 cups frozen mixed berries
2 tablespoons granulated sugar or sugar
  substitute of your choice

2 teaspoons lemon juice
1 sprig fresh rosemary
For Brie
1 9" round Brie cheese wheel

1. Preheat oven to 400°F.

2. To make Compote: In a medium saucepan, combine all ingredients and bring to a simmer over medium heat. Simmer 10 minutes or until slightly thickened. Remove rosemary and set Compote aside.

3. To make Brie: Using a small knife, score top of Brie wheel in a diamond pattern, and place scored-side up in a large cast iron skillet or ceramic baking dish.

4. Place in oven and bake 10–15 minutes until visibly bubbling.

5. Remove cheese from oven, top with Compote, and serve.

COOKING ON SHORT ORDER?

As you're unlikely to live in a comfortable burrow beneath the rolling green, you might, like us, lack a well-stocked country pantry rich with truckles of fine cheese. So, understandably, an entire wheel of Brie can be hard to find with limited time. Let us grant you the luck of the halflings by doubling your odds and letting you know that, yes, this recipe works just as well with Camembert, which is often sold in the wheel size you're looking for.

DWARVEN BATTLE PASTA
Toasted Ravioli

Prep Time: 1 hour, 10 minutes | Cook Time: 15 minutes | Serves 4

Working and residing deep within the caverns riddling ancient mountains means constant threats from tunneling horrors and fearsome goblins. It also means a powerful hunger at the end of the day. Dwarven Battle Pasta is ravioli, carefully toasted to a crispness that will allow it, in a pinch, to be hurled at your monstrous deep-hill neighbors; it also tastes great with a marinara dipping sauce. For an extra cheesy delight, sprinkle the sauce with Parmesan.

3 cups vegetable or other frying oil
3 tablespoons whole milk
2 large eggs
1 cup Italian-style breadcrumbs
¾ teaspoon salt

⅓ cup plus 2 tablespoons grated Parmesan cheese, divided
1 (20-ounce) package frozen ravioli (any fillings)
1 cup warmed marinara sauce

1. Heat oil in deep fryer or large skillet to 350°F.

2. In a small, wide-rimmed bowl, whisk together milk and eggs until smooth. Set aside. Add breadcrumbs, salt, and ⅓ cup Parmesan to a large, sealable bag and shake to combine.

3. Dip frozen ravioli into egg mixture, then add to bag with breadcrumbs and shake to coat.

4. Place a few ravioli at a time into hot oil, cooking about 1 minute on each side until golden brown. Remove from oil to a large paper towel–lined plate. Sprinkle with remaining 2 tablespoons Parmesan before serving alongside warm marinara for dipping.

FRYING TOO GREEDILY AND TOO DEEP

Just a note of warning: Frying ravioli can result in spatters of oil that can burn you, so work slowly and carefully. Remember to dip the pieces into the oil away from you, and fry in small batches so as not to crowd the pan. Dwarves don't fear working right alongside forges, but they also set their beards on fire for dramatic effect, so don't emulate them too closely.

Chapter 2

CLASS-BASED CREATIONS: SNACKS FOR EVERY CHARACTER

Feeling classy? With these stylish recipes, you'll be creating dishes based around all manner of character archetypes with panache and skill. Whether you're looking for something with a flash of steel or a touch of magic, you're sure to find it here. Pick a recipe and take it for a spin for an instant prestige path to character glory.

BARDIC INSTRUMENTS
Za'atar Straws with Labneh

Prep Time: 35 minutes (plus 24 hours cooling time for Labneh)
| Cook Time: 15 minutes | Serves 20

Any bard worth their salt is sure to carry a great many instruments in addition to their favorite, as they never know what manner of ensemble piece they may be called upon to perform. These baked pastry sticks, loaded with the savory, earthy blend of spices known as za'atar, are perfect for when an even mix of coolness and heat is called for—virtues for which most bards are known. Keep a few in your pack, and you'll always be prepared when bardic lore is called for.

For Labneh
1 teaspoon salt
4 cups full-fat plain Greek yogurt
1 tablespoon extra-virgin olive oil

For Straws
½ pound frozen puff pastry, thawed
2 tablespoons extra-virgin olive oil, divided
4 tablespoons za'atar seasoning, divided
1 large egg
2 tablespoons water

1. To make Labneh: In a medium bowl, stir salt into yogurt.

2. Pour mixture onto a clean towel or 2–3 layers of cheesecloth, over a strainer placed over a large bowl. Gather edges of towel or cheesecloth together and twist closed, attaching with a knot, rubber band, or twist tie.

3. Set bowl with mixture in refrigerator 24 hours to thicken. Discard the gathered whey from bowl and check the Labneh consistency before serving, it should be thick and spreadable, similar to Greek yogurt.

4. To make Straws: Preheat oven to 375°F.

5. Place puff pastry on floured work surface. Use a floured rolling pin to roll out into a rectangle about 8" × 12" long and ⅛" thick. Trim edges to even up rectangle.

6. Brush thoroughly with 1 tablespoon oil. Sprinkle 2 tablespoons za'atar seasoning over left half (crosswise) and fold right half over za'atar half.

continued on next page

7. Sprinkle top of pastry with flour and roll out to about 8" × 12" long. Brush remaining 1 tablespoon oil on the left crosswise half, sprinkle with remaining 2 tablespoons za'atar, and fold the right half over. Roll rectangle a few times with rolling pin to seal edges.

8. With a sharp knife, cut pastry lengthwise into ⅓"-wide strips. Twist each strip a few times and place on an ungreased baking sheet. Press the ends down on each strip a little to prevent untwisting in oven.

9. In a small bowl, mix egg with water to create an egg wash. Lightly brush over the top of each strip. Bake 12–15 minutes until Straws are golden brown. Remove and cool 1 minute before serving.

10. In a large, shallow bowl, spread Labneh out, make a small indentation in the center, and fill with 1 tablespoon oil. Serve alongside Straws for dipping.

FASHIONABLE ACCOUTREMENTS

Ever the paragons of style, bards don't miss a trick when it comes to presentation, and their tastes run toward perfection When dressing Labneh, a wide variety of stylish options can take your yogurt dip from basic to bardic. Consider chopped fresh herbs such as marjoram, mint, and flat-leaf parsley, additional za'atar seasoning, chopped pistachios, or a sprinkle of powdered Aleppo pepper to put those impeccable finishing touches on the dish. Your audience will appreciate it.

BEND BARS/CHOP DATES
Oatmeal Date Bars

Prep Time: 25 minutes | Cook Time: 30 minutes | Serves 12

A favorite among the burliest of fighters, barbarians, and any who need that extra bit of fortitude to flex their way out of a jam, these chewy, sweet bars combine the earthiness of oats with the syrupy delicacy of dates to form a powerhouse among cookies. They also pair well with a number of barbarian-beloved drinks, such as nutty ales, cold milk, and the joy of seeing your enemies driven before you.

1½ cups rolled oats
1½ cups sifted pastry flour
¼ teaspoon salt
1⅓ cups packed light brown sugar, divided
¾ teaspoon baking soda

¾ cup unsalted butter, softened
¾ pound pitted and diced dates
1 cup water
1 teaspoon lemon juice

1. Preheat oven to 350°F.

2. In a large bowl, combine oats, flour, salt, 1 cup brown sugar, and baking soda. Add butter and mix until crumbly and moistened. Press half of mixture into the bottom of a 9" square baking pan.

3. In a small saucepan, combine dates, water, and remaining ⅓ cup brown sugar over medium heat. Bring to a boil, and cook until thickened, about 5 minutes. Stir in lemon juice and remove from heat.

4. Spread date mixture in pan, then evenly apply remaining oats mixture on top. Bake 20–25 minutes until top is lightly toasted. Cool 10 minutes before cutting into squares and serving.

FURTHERING THE FORTIFICATION
If the brawlers at your banquet are looking for a little extra protein to pack on their cookie gains, consider adding ½ cup of chopped nuts to the blend during step 3. Just about any nut will contribute well to these bars, but as long as you're baking around feats of strength, the way to go is to crush a few walnuts yourself. With your bare hands, like a titan. Or you can use a nutcracker—your call.

PICKED POCKETS
Bierocks

Prep Time: 2 hours, 30 minutes | Cook Time: 45 minutes | Serves 8

Portable, delicious, and conveniently pocket-sized, these are luscious pockets of spiced meat and cabbage that even the most noble paladin wouldn't begrudge a thief. It'll be easy to nick them the first time, but after everyone at the table has tried them, don't be surprised if the DM doubles the guard in the future.

For Pockets
1 cup room-temperature whole milk
¼ cup granulated sugar
1 (¼-ounce) packet active dry yeast
4 cups unbleached all-purpose flour, divided
2 tablespoons melted salted butter
1 large egg, beaten
¾ teaspoon salt

For Filling
½ pound ground beef
½ large yellow onion, peeled and diced
¼ teaspoon ground cumin
3 cups shredded cabbage
¼ teaspoon salt
¼ teaspoon ground black pepper
1 tablespoon whole milk

1. To make Pockets: In a large bowl, mix milk and sugar until sugar is dissolved. Sprinkle yeast over mixture and let bloom 5–10 minutes until yeast softens and foam starts to appear on the surface.

2. Mix to combine, then whisk in 2 cups flour. Add butter, egg, and salt. Whisk to incorporate.

3. Stir in remaining 2 cups flour ¼ cup at a time until mixture forms a dough. Turn onto a floured work surface and knead 10–15 minutes until a soft, smooth dough forms, adding flour as needed. Dough should be tacky but should not stick to your hands or your kneading surface.

4. Shape dough into a ball, tucking it in on itself toward the bottom to create a rounded top, then place in a large greased bowl, turning to coat. Loosely cover dough with plastic wrap or a damp towel and place in a warm, draft-free place to proof until doubled, about 1 hour.

continued on next page

5. To make Filling: In a large nonstick frying pan over medium heat, cook beef until deeply browned, about 5–7 minutes.

6. Drain grease from pan. Return pan to heat and add onion and cumin. Cook until onion is translucent and beginning to soften, about 3 minutes.

7. Add cabbage and cook an additional 7–10 minutes until cabbage is tender. Remove from heat and season with salt and pepper.

8. Punch air out of risen dough. Divide dough into eight balls and flatten each to a 4" circle.

9. Spoon 2 tablespoons of Filling onto center of each circle. Be sure to leave edges clear of Filling. Bring edges of each dough circle together and pinch them to seal dough completely.

10. Place Bierocks on a greased baking sheet and cover with plastic wrap or a towel to rise 30–45 minutes until about 150 percent their starting size.

11. With 10 minutes of rising time remaining, preheat oven to 375°F.

12. Brush each Bierock lightly with milk and bake 20–25 minutes until golden brown and hollow-sounding when tapped. Remove from oven and cool on a wire rack 15 minutes before serving.

PICKING THE PANTRY'S POCKETS

By now the cannier marks among you will have already kowtowed to the nature of the Picked Pocket, your heads spinning with ideas about all sorts of other possible fillings for these flavor-sealed pouches. And there's plenty to try. Substitute spicy Italian sausage for the ground beef along with a small can of tomato paste, drop the cabbage in favor of chopped mushrooms and some ricotta cheese, and pizza pockets are yours. Cheddar and broccoli works too. Just remember to hold these close in public.

DIAMOND SOUL FOOD
Loaded Breakfast Biscuit

Prep Time: 20 minutes | **Cook Time: 27 minutes** | **Serves 6**

Even the most hardy and stalwart monks feel hunger pangs, and these soulfully loaded biscuits provide the stunning repast any disciple of the fist needs to load up on calories and Ki for a long day's adventuring work.

1 pound ground breakfast sausage
2½ cups all-purpose flour
1 tablespoon baking powder
¾ teaspoon salt

4 tablespoons melted salted butter, divided
4 large eggs, beaten
1 cup shredded sharp Cheddar cheese
⅔ cup low-fat milk

1. Preheat oven to 425°F.

2. In a 12" cast iron skillet, cook sausage over medium heat until browned through, about 7 minutes. Drain.

3. In a large bowl, combine flour, baking powder, and salt. Add cooked sausage and stir to combine. Set aside.

4. Add 2 tablespoons butter and eggs to skillet used for sausage and cook to a soft scramble, about 5 minutes. Add to sausage mixture and stir to combine.

5. Add cheese and milk and stir mixture until all flour is incorporated and a slightly sticky dough forms.

6. Using a spoon, floured hands, or an ice cream scoop, drop biscuits into twelve even scoops onto a large, buttered skillet or baking sheet. Bake 12–15 minutes until biscuits are lightly golden brown and a toothpick inserted into the center comes out clean.

7. Brush tops of hot biscuits with remaining 2 tablespoons butter. Serve warm.

COMBO POTENTIAL
Try pairing these already decadent biscuits with a peppery milk gravy to create the ultimate plate of biscuits and gravy. Taboo? That's up to you.

BARBARIAN GREATCLUB
Bacon-Wrapped Smoky Turkey Leg

Prep Time: 10 minutes | Cook Time: 1 hour, 30 minutes | Serves 1

Barbarous warriors from far in the frozen reaches of the North are nothing if not practical. Actually, wait, they're barbarous. So they're nothing if not barbarous and practical. Also hungry. Barbarous, practical, and hungry. So it was only a matter of time before some enterprising warrior thought to just take dinner onto the battlefield and brain some foes with it. The results? A colossal club of turkey and bacon, perfect for snacking between snacks, able to quell the rage within and replace it with a satisfying sleepiness. It's the ultimate in primal dinner.

1 (2-pound) turkey leg
½ teaspoon salt, divided
⅛ teaspoon ground black pepper, divided
9 strips regular-cut bacon

1 tablespoon olive oil
1 tablespoon maple syrup
1 teaspoon smoked paprika
1 teaspoon garlic powder, divided

1. Preheat oven to 350°F.

2. Coat turkey leg with ¼ teaspoon salt and 1/16 teaspoon pepper, then wrap tightly in bacon.

3. In a small bowl, combine oil, maple syrup, paprika, garlic powder, and remaining ¼ teaspoon salt and 1/16 teaspoon pepper. Set aside half of mixture and brush the remaining half over the bacon.

4. Place turkey leg on an ungreased baking sheet and bake 1 hour. Remove from oven and brush on remaining syrup mixture. Bake an additional 30 minutes until the bacon is cooked crisp.

5. Cool turkey leg on a wire rack 10 minutes before serving.

BRING ALONG THE TRIBE

The serving size for this recipe will seem a little silly once you're presented with one of these massive installations of weaponized protein, but barbarians are nothing if not ambitious (yes, and barbarous, practical, and hungry). The good news is that this recipe couldn't be easier to double, triple, and more to feed a hungry table or a hungry warband.

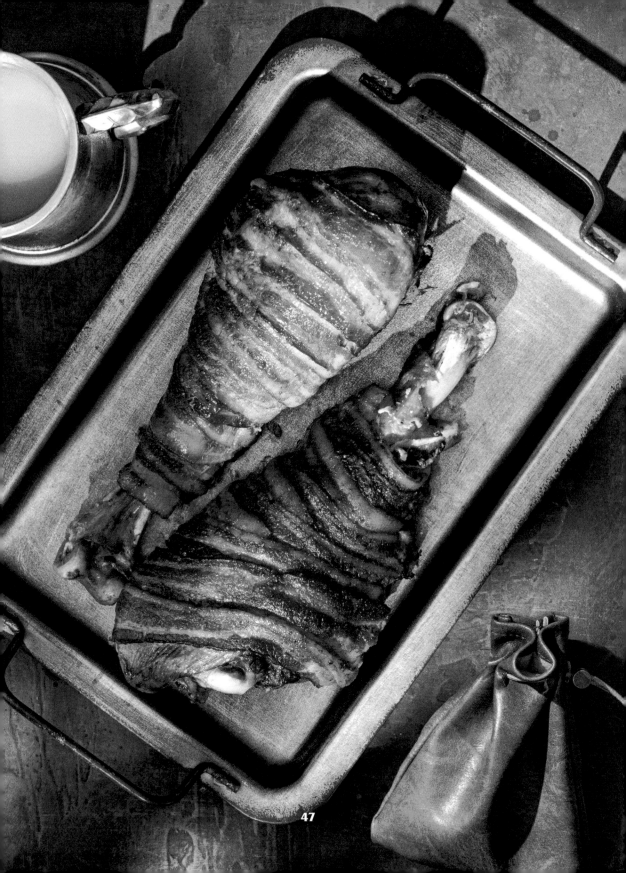

HARVEST-TIME HELPERS
Pumpkin Cinnamon Rolls

Prep Time: 2 hours, 30 minutes | Cook Time: 28 minutes | Serves 12

Harvest time can be a difficult season for fantasy villagers. Sure, there's the promise of food to last through a harsh winter, but also there's bugbears and such. That's where adventurers tend to come in: to keep the fearsome invaders and desperate thieves at bay. When the hard work is complete and the goblinoids have been driven back to the hills, it's time to face a simple economic truth: Adventurers are always impossibly wealthier than fantasy farm folk. So how does this mutual assistance program work? Through incredibly delicious Pumpkin Cinnamon Rolls, obviously. Adventurers can barely get through reheating lembas bread by themselves.

For Rolls
3¼ cups all-purpose flour, divided
1 (¼-ounce) packet active dry yeast
½ cup canned pumpkin
⅔ cup whole milk
4 tablespoons room-temperature unsalted butter, divided
2 tablespoons granulated sugar
½ teaspoon salt
1 large egg, beaten
½ cup packed light brown sugar
1 teaspoon ground cinnamon

For Frosting
2 tablespoons room-temperature unsalted butter
¼ cup packed light brown sugar
1 tablespoon whole milk
⅓ cup confectioners' sugar, divided
¼ teaspoon vanilla extract
⅛ teaspoon salt

1. **To make Rolls:** In a large bowl, combine 1½ cups flour with yeast and set aside.

2. In a medium saucepan, combine pumpkin, milk, 2 tablespoons butter, granulated sugar, and salt over medium heat until warmed and butter is almost melted, about 3 minutes.

3. Add egg and contents of saucepan to flour mixture and use an electric mixer to beat on low speed 30 seconds. Increase speed to high and beat 3 minutes. Continue adding remaining 1¾ cups flour to mixture until a firm, tacky dough forms.

4. Knead dough on a lightly floured surface until smooth and elastic, roughly 6–8 minutes. Place dough in a large greased bowl, turning to coat. Cover with plastic wrap or a towel and let rise until doubled in size, about 1 hour.

5. Roll dough out on a lightly floured work surface into a 1" × 10" rectangle. In a microwave-safe small bowl, melt remaining 2 table-spoons butter in microwave 40 seconds on high, then brush onto dough surface. In a separate small bowl, combine brown sugar and cinnamon and sprinkle over dough.

6. Roll dough into a jelly roll shape, starting from the long side. Cut into twelve slices. Place Rolls cut-side down in a greased 13" × 9" baking pan. Cover and let rise until doubled in size again, about 30 minutes.

7. While the dough is rising, preheat oven to 375°F.

8. Bake Rolls 20–25 minutes until golden brown, then cool on a wire rack 15 minutes.

9. To make Frosting: In a medium saucepan, melt butter over medium-low heat, then stir in brown sugar and milk. Cook and stir 1 minute. Stir in ¼ cup confectioners' sugar, vanilla, and salt, mixing until smooth. If the mixture is too thin or runny, continue stirring in small amounts of confectioners' sugar until desired consistency is achieved.

10. Drizzle Frosting over Rolls and serve warm.

ROAD ROLLS

One of the great delights involved in setting out for defense of the simple farmlands is the big basket of treats the locals send along; the Harvest-Time Helpers are a big highlight of this mobile feast. Just keep an eye on them, since the last thing any adventurer wants to do is tell the town guard that yes, actually, someone *did* steal their sweetroll.

HELLFIRE HOT WINGS
Spicy Mango Oven Hot Wings

Prep Time: 45 minutes | Cook Time: 1 hour, 5 minutes | Serves 2

Through dark pacts made with beings beyond understanding or reason, warlocks learn to channel terrible hellfires that burn through armor, magic, and bone like so much kindling. Understandably, they are often loath to practice this magic with cooking, but a slight tendency toward recklessness is, of course, part of any good dark bargainer's makeup. Thus is born the Hellfire Hot Wing, cursed with searing heat but cloaked in a tempting offer of syrupy mango sweetness. Feel the burn!

½ cup all-purpose flour
½ teaspoon chili powder
½ teaspoon garlic powder
½ teaspoon ground black pepper
½ teaspoon salt
1 pound (about 5–6) chicken wings
1 medium mango, peeled

3 habanero peppers, seeded
2 cloves garlic, peeled
½ teaspoon paprika
¼ cup apple cider vinegar
2 tablespoons lime juice
¼ cup honey

1. Preheat oven to 425°F.

2. In a small bowl, combine flour, chili powder, garlic powder, black pepper, and salt.

3. Use a paper towel to pat chicken wings dry. Dredge wings in flour mixture and set on a wire rack placed on a rimmed baking sheet.

4. Bake 45 minutes, flipping halfway through for even cooking. Remove from oven and set aside.

5. In a blender, combine mango, habanero peppers, garlic, paprika, vinegar, and lime juice.

6. In a medium saucepan, cook mango habanero mix and honey over medium heat. Stir occasionally to prevent sticking and simmer 5–10 minutes or until sauce reaches preferred consistency. Remove from heat.

continued on next page

7. Increase oven temperature to 450°F. Fully coat cooked wings in sauce, then place on a parchment paper–lined baking sheet.

8. Bake 8–10 minutes until sauce has slightly caramelized. Remove from oven and cool wings 5 minutes on a wire rack before serving.

PACT WITH FLAVOR

Though warlocks are prone to heedlessly agree to a short-term bargain in exchange for overwhelming force, you don't have to make their mistakes. Remember to wear gloves when seeding and chopping habanero peppers, don't touch your skin with their juices, and have plenty of milk on hand when tasting. If you're truly terrified of Scoville realms beyond our understanding, substitute jalapeños.

MULTICLASSIC SALAD
Gnocchi German Potato Salad

Prep Time: 15 minutes | **Cook Time: 30 minutes (plus time to boil gnocchi)** | **Serves 6**

Can't decide between fighter and wizard for your character? Enjoy the best of both worlds with multiclassing, the gish's favorite tool to mix swords and sorcery, thieving and barding, and nobility with curses from the olden days. The Multiclassic Salad brings this same energy to your table. Why choose between pasta and potato salad when you can just have both? Gnocchi lends this dish a toothsome chew, and while the bacon and onions decry the very concept of salad, there's enough parsley here to appease skeptics looking for at least one green thing.

1 large white onion, peeled and cut into
  thick slices
4 strips thick-cut bacon
1 pound gnocchi
¼ cup apple cider vinegar
1 tablespoon good-quality mustard,
  such as brown horseradish

½ teaspoon kosher salt
½ teaspoon granulated sugar
½ teaspoon freshly cracked black pepper
¼ teaspoon celery seed
½ cup plus 2 tablespoons chopped fresh
  parsley, divided

1. Preheat oven to 425°F. In a large roasting pan, scatter onion in a single even layer, then add bacon on top without overlapping strips.

2. Bake 20–30 minutes until bacon is crispy.

3. While onion is cooking, boil a large pot of well-salted water over high heat.

4. Remove pan from oven, move bacon to a large, paper towel–lined plate, and pour off bacon fat into a small bowl, reserving for later.

5. Boil gnocchi according to package directions, then drain and add to pan with onion. Stir in 2 tablespoons reserved bacon fat to coat.

6. In a small bowl, stir together vinegar, mustard, salt, sugar, pepper, and celery seed. Add vinegar mixture to gnocchi and onion, stirring and scraping onion bits up from bottom of pan.

continued on next page

7. Roughly chop bacon and add it along with ½ cup parsley to the pan and stir. Transfer to a serving bowl, top with remaining 2 tablespoons parsley, and serve.

DUAL CLASSICS

If you're a truly old-school gamer, you may be missing some of the more classic elements of salad design, namely all that mayo. Gnocchi are versatile and will lend themselves well to a more traditional American-style potato salad, if you prefer. Once you've experienced the versatility of this hack, you'll rarely venture back to the old way.

BREAKFAST FOR PALADINNER
Eggs Benedict Burgers

Prep Time: 15 minutes | Cook Time: 21 minutes | Serves 4

Paladins historically must tithe some portion of all their hard-earned adventuring spoils to the church so as to maintain the holy works of the priests, and to ensure that paladins maintain some sense of piety and humility while traveling. In order to prepare for this eventual tightening of their belts, holy warriors like to fill up on breakfast. Or dinner, frankly. Just leave the Detect Evil spell off, because this combination of Eggs Benedict and a juicy hamburger is at the very least a little decadent, if not outright sinful.

1½ pounds ground beef
½ teaspoon salt
¼ teaspoon ground black pepper
4 hamburger buns, halved
1 (1¼-ounce) packet hollandaise sauce mix
1 cup whole milk

1½ teaspoons stone-ground mustard
6 strips thick-cut bacon
4 large eggs
4 large romaine lettuce leaves
4 slices large beefsteak tomato

1. In a large bowl, combine beef, salt, and pepper, working lightly so as not to overmix. Shape beef into four ½"-thick patties, using your thumb to press a dimple into the center of each patty.

2. Over medium-high heat on a grill or in a large skillet on the stovetop, cook burgers, covered, over medium heat 4–6 minutes on each side to desired doneness. While burgers cook, toast buns.

3. In a small bowl, prepare the hollandaise sauce according to instructions, using sauce mix, milk, and mustard.

4. Heat a large nonstick skillet coated with cooking spray over medium-high heat, and cook bacon to desired doneness (8–15 minutes). Remove from pan (saving the bacon grease) and set on a large, paper towel–lined plate to drain before cutting each strip in half crosswise.

5. Break eggs one by one into skillet with bacon grease, then reduce heat to low. Cook until whites are set (5–6 minutes), and turn once, if desired.

6. Dress each bottom bun with lettuce, tomato, bacon, and a burger patty, then top patty with sauce, egg, and remaining bun half. Serve hot.

A MEAL WORTH FALLING FOR

The Breakfast for Paladinner is practically a meal in and of itself, capable of leaving any paladin feeling like they could simply fall, and maybe lie on their hands for a while. Before consuming, check with your DM to see if your paladin disease immunity covers feelings of fullness and occasional heartburn, and be prepared with a healing spell or antacid as necessary.

Chapter 3

APPETIZING ABILITIES: FOOD FOR FEATS

Spells, feats, attacks, prayers, and exploits. Whatever you call them, these are the tools that adventurers use to separate the dashing fighter from the somewhat more mundane soldier. We've taken a few of the coolest abilities that a character can use and transformed them into feats you can accomplish yourself in your own kitchen. Dazzle your friend and improve your parties without having to resort to wish spells…or delivery. Follow our steps here, and you'll have everything you need to create the tools of the trade!

SPENSER'S MINTY DISCS
Melted Mint Cookies

Prep Time: 2 hours, 10 minutes | Cook Time: 21 minutes | Yields 80 cookies

Created by the beloved brother of a somewhat more copyrighted wizard, these exceptionally easy cookies combine rich chocolate with the zing of mint in a way that screams holiday cheer, but that's no reason to save them for the wintertime. Sure, they may not float your belongings a few feet above the ground, but you'll feel like you're floating with every bite.

1 pound (about 96 pieces) Andes or other green chocolate wafer mints, unwrapped
¾ cup cold unsalted butter or margarine
1½ cups packed dark brown sugar
2 tablespoons water

1 (12-ounce) package semisweet chocolate chips
2 large eggs
2½ cups all-purpose flour
1¼ teaspoons baking soda
½ teaspoon salt

1. In a large bowl, place mints, breaking each into large chunks if you have fewer than eighty mints.

2. In a medium-sized heavy saucepan, heat butter, brown sugar, and water over low heat until butter is melted, about 3–5 minutes. Add chocolate chips and cook, stirring continuously until partially melted, about 3 minutes. Remove from heat and stir until chocolate is completely melted.

3. Pour mixture into a large bowl and let stand 10 minutes to cool. Use an electric mixer to beat in eggs, one at a time, on medium speed until thoroughly combined.

4. Reduce speed to low and add flour, baking soda, and salt, beating until just blended. Refrigerate dough 1 hour.

5. With 10 minutes of refrigeration remaining, preheat oven to 350°F.

6. Line two baking sheets with aluminum foil. Roll balls of cookie dough (about 1 teaspoon in size) and place 2" apart on prepared baking sheets.

continued on next page

7. Bake 12–13 minutes until just set and tops of cookies are beginning to crack. Remove from oven and immediately place 1 mint or mint piece on top of each hot cookie. Let mint soften, then swirl over cookie with a skewer to frost.

8. Transfer cookies to wire racks to cool completely before serving, about 15 minutes or until mint frosting is set and solid.

FLOATING DISC IDEAS

If you're having trouble finding wafer mints, fear not! There's a plethora of excellent replacement melty toppings, though the low melting point of the wafer mints makes them easier to work with. You can substitute with one Hershey's Kisses Candy Cane per cookie; you'll just need to babysit the melting process a little, standing by with a skewer and swirling the mint until it pools. Cherry cordials or other flavored chocolate will also work, for the rare attendee of a game night who simply can't stand mint.

SLOW SPELLS
Cheese Dreams

Prep Time: 30 minutes | Cook Time: 15 minutes | Serves 16

These elevated little grilled cheese sandwich delights are so rich, they'll slow down even the twitchiest adventurer to savor their sharp and nutty balance. If you find your table in need of a relaxed pace for an evening, consider a tray of these, coupled with an "accidental" lapse in soda prep. You'll be forgiven by the second bite.

2 cups finely grated sharp Cheddar cheese
1 cup softened salted butter
2 tablespoons heavy cream
1 large egg
1 teaspoon Worcestershire sauce

½ teaspoon salt
½ teaspoon dry mustard
¼ teaspoon ground red pepper
16 slices firm white sandwich bread,
  crusts removed

1. Preheat oven to 375°F.

2. In a medium bowl, use an electric mixer to beat cheese and butter on medium speed until well blended. Beat in cream, egg, Worcestershire, salt, mustard, and red pepper.

3. Cut each bread slice into four squares. Spread cheese mixture on half of bread squares, using about 1 teaspoon per square. Top each with another bread square. Spread remaining cheese mixture over top and sides of sandwiches.

4. Place sandwiches 1" apart on a lightly greased baking sheet and bake 15 minutes or until golden brown. Serve on a large platter.

HASTE SPELLS?
Need to counteract the somnolent effects of Slow? First of all, don't worry overmuch; the effects are temporary and will disappear after a few hours' rest or a single critical hit at a clutch moment. But in the case of a true emergency, consider a cup of coffee or six.

TRANSMUTE STONE TO PIZZA
Pepperoni Pizza Dip

Prep Time: 15 minutes | Cook Time: 20 minutes | Serves 8

Certainly this spell can be cast on perfectly round stone discs to create a more traditional pizza, but perfectly round stone discs are harder to obtain than delivery, unless, of course, you're in the para-elemental plane of perfectly round stone discs (between the quasi-elemental plane of platonic solids and the pepperoni aethereum).

1 (8-ounce) package softened
 cream cheese
½ cup sour cream
1 teaspoon dried oregano
¼ teaspoon garlic salt

1 (12-ounce) jar pizza sauce
1 (6-ounce) package pepperoni slices
1 cup shredded mozzarella cheese
1 teaspoon Italian seasoning

1. Preheat oven to 350°F.

2. In a medium bowl, combine cream cheese, sour cream, oregano, and garlic salt. Spread mixture into the bottom of a 9" pie pan or square baking dish.

3. Spread pizza sauce evenly over cream cheese mixture, then top with pepperoni slices. Bake 10 minutes.

4. Remove from oven. Quickly top with mozzarella cheese and more pepperoni slices. Return to oven to bake 7–8 minutes until cheese is melted.

5. Turn oven to high broil and cook 1–2 minutes until cheese is dotted with brown and pepperoni slices crisp up a bit.

6. Remove from oven and sprinkle Italian seasoning over top. Serve hot.

METAMAGIC OPTIONS

Transmute Stone to Pizza is best served alongside pita chips, sliced baguette, or any other dip tool you're partial to. Looking to maximize flavor? Add your favorite pizza toppings to take this dish to the next level! Consider roasted garlic, chopped red onion, bell pepper, and more.

TOUCH OF DEATH
Bones of the Dead Cookies

Prep Time: 40 minutes | Cook Time: 15 minutes | Yields about 36 cookies

Necromancers may be devious and driven to the dark arts, but their baking skills are above reproach, especially once they've amassed a little potency and a couple of skeletal sous chefs. Derived from a traditional Italian holiday cookie, these little ossuary sweets are dangerous if you fail your save against eating far too many. At that point, they'll reduce your motivation to zero, leaving you unable to continue in the adventure except to acquire more cookies.

3 tablespoons softened unsalted butter
1¼ cups granulated sugar
1 large egg white
1 teaspoon vanilla extract
1½ cups all-purpose flour
½ cup whole-wheat flour

½ cup ground almonds
Zest of 1 medium lemon
1 teaspoon ground cinnamon
¼ teaspoon ground cloves
1 tablespoon Italian liqueur or white wine
¼ cup confectioners' sugar

1. Line three baking sheets with parchment paper.

2. In a large bowl, use an electric mixer to cream together butter and granulated sugar on medium speed until smooth and creamy.

3. In a small bowl, whisk together egg and vanilla. Add egg mixture to butter mixture and beat on medium speed 1–2 minutes until combined.

4. In a separate small bowl, combine both kinds of flour, almonds, lemon zest, cinnamon, and cloves.

5. Slowly add flour mixture to butter mixture on medium speed until combined, pausing mixer occasionally to scrape down sides of bowl.

6. Add liqueur or white wine and mix. If the dough is not fully smooth and tacky to the touch, add 1 more tablespoon liqueur or wine.

7. Remove dough from bowl and wrap tightly in plastic wrap. Refrigerate 45 minutes.

8. While dough is chilling, preheat oven to 350°F.

9. Lightly flour a clean work surface or cutting board. Cut chilled dough into four pieces. Roll one piece into a rope 18" long. Cut into two halves. Cut one half into cookies that are about 3" long and ½" thick. Line them up on one prepared baking sheet with some space (at least 1") between them. Press down a little on each cookie. Continue the process with remaining dough on remaining prepared baking sheets.

10. Bake 15 minutes or until edges just start to turn golden brown. Remove from oven and immediately dust with confectioners' sugar. Cool completely before serving, about 30 minutes.

A DEATHLY CRUMBLE

Like bones, Touches of Death are a bit crisp and crunchy, crumbly by design, and serve well as dipping implements. While a true necromancer will generally wish to dunk their confectionery in the ichor of the freshly damned, coffee will also work in a pinch.

HEALING WORDS
Lavender Honey Cupcakes

Prep Time: 35 minutes | Cook Time: 24 minutes | Yields 12 cupcakes

A gentle, sweet delight, these cupcakes house all the healing power of a potion, but unlike a healing draft, their honey richness and light lavender frosting are instantly recognizable and appreciated, whereas a healing potion, like fruit punch of dubious provenance, just tastes... red. Do note that consuming a cupcake isn't a free or bonus action. Sprinkle your Healing Words with extra lavender buds for a stunning finish.

For Cupcakes
½ cup softened unsalted butter
1 cup granulated sugar
2 large eggs
2 teaspoons vanilla extract
1 teaspoon red food coloring
1 teaspoon blue food coloring
1½ cups all-purpose flour
½ teaspoon baking powder
¼ teaspoon salt
2½ tablespoons finely chopped dried
 lavender buds
⅔ cup cold whole milk

For Frosting
½ cup softened unsalted butter
1 (8-ounce) package softened
 cream cheese
4 cups confectioners' sugar
2 teaspoons vanilla extract
3 tablespoons honey, divided
2 drops red food coloring
1 drop blue food coloring

1. To make Cupcakes: Preheat oven to 350°F. Line a twelve-cup muffin tin with paper liners.

2. In a large bowl, use an electric mixer to cream together butter and granulated sugar on medium speed until smooth and combined. Reduce speed to low and add eggs one at a time. Mix in vanilla and food coloring.

3. In a medium bowl, combine flour, baking powder, and salt. Stir in lavender buds.

continued on next page

4. Slowly pour flour mixture into butter mixture while mixing on low speed. Slowly add milk, still mixing on low, until just combined and no lumps remain.

5. Spoon batter evenly into muffin tin cups, filling each liner to ⅔ full. Bake 18–24 minutes until a toothpick inserted in the center comes out clean. Cool cupcakes in tin 10 minutes, then transfer to a wire rack to cool completely, about 20 minutes.

6. **To make Frosting:** After cleaning the mixing bowl, use an electric mixer to beat butter and cream cheese on medium speed until smooth and creamy.

7. Reduce speed to low and add confectioners' sugar 1 cup at a time until Frosting is smooth and creamy. Beat in vanilla and 2 tablespoons honey until fully combined. Stir in food colorings to desired color.

8. Pipe or spread Frosting onto cooled cupcakes, then drizzle remaining 1 tablespoon honey over tops before serving.

HONEYED WORDS OF CAUTION

Sure, it's fun to compare these delightful cakes to healing potions, but be warned, potions have a significant advantage over cupcakes in certain hit point recovery situations. Healing Words are not to be administered to anyone who has fallen below 1 HP, as you won't impart any healing. You'll just render their face all sticky.

GOODBERRIES, EXCEPT THEY'RE DATES
Cheesy Bacon-Wrapped Dates

Prep Time: 15 minutes | **Cook Time: 10 minutes** | **Yields 16 dates**

Druids routinely prepare for long journeys with a brace of healing berries, magically infused with such intense energy that a single berry has the calories needed for a whole day's work. While that recipe is a closely guarded secret, a spell, and also impossible, this delectable appetizer seeks to also pack an incredible amount of richness and sustenance into a delightful fruity package.

16 dates, pitted and sliced open
  lengthwise

16 ounces Gruyère cheese, chopped
16 strips regular-cut bacon

1. Preheat oven to 375°F.

2. Insert a small amount of cheese into each date and press sides together to close.

3. Wrap each date in 1 strip bacon, then arrange on a wire rack placed on a baking sheet and bake 8–10 minutes until bacon is crisp.

4. Remove from oven. Skewer each date with a toothpick and place on a large, paper towel–lined plate. Allow to drain 5 minutes before serving.

THESE DATES ARE FLEXIBLE

Gruyère is certainly the classic option, but it isn't the only one. You can definitely experiment with all sorts of cheese, from sharp Cheddar to raclette. Anything you might normally pair with bacon will work well here. That said, a true druid will know to avoid processed American cheese in this application, since it's designed to melt and scorch black in the oven in moments. Besides, it's unnatural. This isn't a warlock recipe.

WHIRLWIND ATTACKS
Goat Cheese and Herb Pinwheels

Prep Time: 20 minutes | Cook Time: 15 minutes | Serves 12

Looking for a snack that's not just a hit but a hit with everyone at the table at the same time? Leap into the fray armed with these oven-baked puff pastry classics, and you'll immediately be at the center of a whirlwind of praise and happiness, without even having to complete the feat chain. As easy to dish up as they are to dish out (damage), these cheesy, garlicky hors d'oeuvres will leave your gathering ready to come and get it.

1 cup goat cheese
4 tablespoons whipping cream
1 tablespoon finely minced garlic
2 tablespoons chopped fresh
flat-leaf parsley

2 tablespoons chopped fresh basil
1 teaspoon freshly crushed black pepper
2 sheets frozen puff pastry, thawed

1. Preheat oven to 400°F. Line a baking sheet with parchment paper.

2. In a medium bowl, mix together all ingredients except puff pastry.

3. On a lightly floured cutting board or work surface, cut puff pastry into ½"-wide strips. Twist two pieces together in a tight spiral and place flat on prepared baking sheet.

4. Spoon 1 rounded teaspoonful of goat cheese mixture on each pinwheel. Bake 15 minutes or until golden brown. Serve immediately.

OTHER TOPPING FEATS

To quickly convert this recipe from Whirlwind Attacks to Spring Attacks, simply substitute an equal part of feta for goat cheese, and some springy herbs and veggies for the basil and parsley. Ramps, chives, or green onions, tossed with thyme or rosemary, will accomplish this easy shift. Don't skip the garlic, though; that's a crowd-pleaser in any presentation.

PIERCING BLADES
Teriyaki Chicken Skewers

Prep Time: 45 minutes | Cook Time: 13 minutes | Serves 4

Among certain fantasy cultures, it's considered honorable and polite to peacebond one's sword in town, tying it off in the scabbard as a gesture of peaceful intent and goodwill. This is certainly a tasteful display, but if you want something tasty instead, consider sheathing your blades in tangy marinated chicken and fresh fruits and vegetables, and cloaking them in the fires of the forge until everything is tender and delicious. It may not be as formal as a peacebond, but we believe you'll still make more friends this way.

½ cup packed light brown sugar
½ cup soy sauce
¼ cup pineapple juice
2 cloves garlic, peeled and minced
¼ teaspoon ground black pepper
½ teaspoon salt
1 tablespoon water
1 tablespoon cornstarch
4 (6-ounce) boneless, skinless chicken
 breasts, cut into 1" cubes

1 medium red bell pepper, seeded and
 cut into 1" cubes
1 medium yellow bell pepper, seeded
 and cut into 1" cubes
1 medium green bell pepper, seeded and
 cut into 1" cubes
1 medium red onion, peeled and cut into
 1" cubes
2 cups 1" cubes fresh pineapple
2 tablespoons chopped green onions

1. In a small saucepan over medium heat, whisk together brown sugar, soy sauce, pineapple juice, garlic, pepper, and salt.

2. In a small bowl, whisk together water and cornstarch. Slowly whisk into soy sauce mixture.

3. Bring soy sauce mixture to boil over medium-high heat 1–3 minutes until mixture just starts to thicken. Remove from heat and reserve ¼ cup.

4. In a large bowl, marinate chicken in remaining sauce. Set in refrigerator at least 30 minutes, up to 4 hours.

5. About 15 minutes before cooking, preheat grill to medium heat.

continued on next page

6. Thread marinated chicken onto skewers, alternating with the peppers, red onion, and pineapple.

7. Grill over medium heat 8–10 minutes until meat reaches internal temperature of 165°F and juices run clear. Remove from grill and baste with reserved sauce mixture. Garnish with green onions and serve.

YOU CAN STAB ANYTHING ONCE

Chicken may be the main event in these skewers, but the flavors of teriyaki mix well with nearly any vegetable, fruit, or edible fungus, so feel free to explore options when assembling your station. Toss in some button mushrooms or cubed portobello, substitute peach or watermelon for the pineapple (or just do all three), and you'll still have a greatsword (of flavors).

CRITICAL DIP
Peach Lime Salsa

Prep Time: 15 minutes | **Cook Time: N/A** | **Yields about 1½ cups**

Game tables are rarely complete without a bag or two of chips being passed around. Sure, it's easy to just buy some salsa at the store and call it a day. However, salsa is a deeply personal matter to some, with such details as thickness, spice level, and salt all precariously balancing the dip between victory and mushy defeat. If you'd like to succeed every time, and succeed for double damage, try this critically acclaimed salsa. It'll be a hit! The kind that does double damage.

4 large ripe peaches, peeled, pitted,
 and diced
½ large red bell pepper, seeded and diced
¼ cup peeled and diced red onion
1 medium jalapeño, seeded and minced
Zest and juice of 1 medium lime

1 tablespoon honey
2 tablespoons chopped fresh cilantro
½ teaspoon hot sauce
⅛ teaspoon salt
⅛ teaspoon ground black pepper

In a large bowl, combine all ingredients, then cover with plastic wrap and set aside at least 1 hour or up to overnight before serving.

FIERY BURST ON CRIT?

As far as salsa dangers go, this is a tame and peach-forward affair, the spice equivalent of a couple of kobolds guarding a chest. If you feel the need for further heat, there's a wide variety of options available. Leave in the jalapeño seeds, double the jalapeño, or even add a diced habanero pepper to the party. That'll take this encounter from beginner to epic in a hurry, the salsa version of a roaring dragon on the rim of a volcano.

Chapter 4

THE MAGIC ITEM TABLE:
NOSHES FOR MAGICAL MARVELS

Fresh Fruit

HOT
POPPER
DIP!

Ah, the great reward at the end of any good adventure, a few rolls on the big table of awesome glowing loot. Will it be another boring scroll of Identify, or is today the day you're going to finally get that awesome Trident of Fish Command? In this chapter, we take a few of the classic bits of spectacular rewards you might earn and carefully re-create them in food form, so you don't even need to roll anymore. You get the best stuff, and you get to eat it too!

NECKLACE OF FIREBALLS
Coconut Chicken Nuggets with Tropical Sauce

Prep Time: 20 minutes | Cook Time: 15 minutes | Serves 8

Looking for a wizard's artillery without all the studying? You're in luck, as wizards throughout history have always seemed to display a frankly shocking lack of foresight, flooding the world with powerful artifacts that replicate their carefully learned abilities for just anyone to fling around. One such device is the terrifying necklace of fireballs, capable of hurling explosive bursts across the battlefield with wild abandon. We've replicated the heat and structure here, replacing most of the chance of death with tender chicken and coconut.

For Sauce
¼ cup sweet chili sauce
¼ cup apricot preserves

For Nuggets
3 large eggs
½ cup whole milk
1½ cups all-purpose flour, divided
1 (7-ounce) package shredded coconut
2 teaspoons cayenne pepper
½ teaspoon ground dried chipotle pepper
2 cups vegetable oil
2½ pounds boneless, skinless chicken
breasts, cut into 1" chunks

1. To make Sauce: In a small bowl, mix all ingredients together, then cover and refrigerate until ready to serve.

2. To make Nuggets: In a large, wide-rimmed bowl, beat eggs. Add milk, ¾ cup flour, and coconut and continue to beat to create a batter.

3. In a separate large, wide-rimmed bowl, mix together remaining ¾ cup flour with cayenne and chipotle pepper.

4. In a large skillet, heat 1" of oil over medium-high heat to 350°F.

5. Dip chicken pieces in flour mixture, then batter, keeping moisture out of flour mixture from one piece to the next, using the wet/dry method (use one hand for only batter dredging, the other for flour dredging).

continued on next page

6. Carefully add nuggets in batches small enough that they aren't touching in the skillet (ten or so at a time) to hot oil and fry until golden brown, about 5 minutes. Remove to a wire rack over paper towels to drain and cool. Repeat with remaining nuggets. Serve hot alongside Sauce.

NECKLACE OF REGULAR BALLS?

First of all, ew. But sure, go for it. If you're a natural-born spice dodger, this recipe will function just fine without the peppers, especially since the sauce is still there to provide tanginess and zip. No self-respecting wizard would just fling their balls around unfired, but improvisation is the soul of adventure!

THE CAULDRON OF EVERYTHING GOOD
Jalapeño Popper Dip

Prep Time: 30 minutes | Cook Time: 45 minutes | Serves 8

A deep, bubbling vessel swirling with bacon, garlic, and jalapeño, barely visible under the crackling patina of cheese and breadcrumbs heaped over the top, the Cauldron of Everything Good is superior to most D&D cauldrons in just about every way.

For Dip
8 strips thick-cut bacon
2 (8-ounce) packages room-temperature
 cream cheese
1 cup mayonnaise
6 medium jalapeños, seeded and minced
2 cloves garlic, peeled and minced

½ teaspoon ground cumin
1½ cups shredded Cheddar cheese
For Topping
1 cup panko breadcrumbs
1 cup grated Parmesan cheese
4 tablespoons melted unsalted butter

1. Preheat oven to 375°F.

2. To make Dip: In a large nonstick skillet, cook bacon in batches over medium-high heat until crisp, about 12–15 minutes. Transfer to a large, paper towel–lined plate to cool, about 5 minutes, then roughly chop into small pieces.

3. In a large bowl, combine cream cheese, mayonnaise, jalapeños, garlic, cumin, and Cheddar with bacon. Pour into a 13" × 9" baking dish.

4. To make Topping: In a small bowl, combine breadcrumbs, Parmesan, and butter, tossing until breadcrumbs are evenly moistened. Sprinkle evenly over cream cheese mixture.

5. Bake 25–30 minutes until top is golden brown and Dip is bubbling. Remove from oven and let rest 5 minutes before serving.

THE LEVEL DIP
Chips, French bread, vegetables, and other delicious dippables will all turn this dish from a magic item to an artifact powerful enough to leave you with an ego score.

PHILTER OF LOVE
Strawberry Buttermilk Snowballs

Prep Time: 25 minutes | Cook Time: 5 minutes | Serves 2

The classic magical Philter of Love is nothing short of a love potion, charming the imbiber to fall in love with the first creature they see for at least an hour. A terrifying concoction, the original has been modified to replace certain uncomfortable undertones with something everyone can enjoy: strawberries and custard.

1½ cups buttermilk
3 large egg yolks
¼ cup plus ¼ teaspoon granulated sugar, divided

½ teaspoon vanilla extract
⅛ teaspoon salt
1 cup hulled and sliced fresh strawberries
4 cups ice cubes

1. In a medium saucepan, whisk buttermilk, egg yolks, and ¼ cup sugar, then cook over medium-high heat while whisking constantly until mixture is thick enough to coat the back of a spoon, about 4–5 minutes.

2. Remove from heat, whisk in vanilla and salt, then transfer to a large measuring cup or bowl. Cover and refrigerate 15 minutes.

3. In a small bowl, sprinkle remaining ¼ teaspoon sugar over strawberries and toss to coat. Cover bowl and let sit at room temperature 10 minutes.

4. Add ice to a blender and blend using the Crush setting until ice is blended to consistency of loose snow.

5. Pour 3 tablespoons of refrigerated custard into the bottom of two pint glasses, followed by 1 tablespoon strawberries, then enough crushed ice to cover strawberries. Repeat layers until glasses are full. Serve immediately with long-handled spoons.

LOVE IS SOMETIMES MESSY

A pint glass heaped high with custard, shaved ice, and strawberries, the Philter of Love can be a daunting dessert to conquer alone. Make sure to bring napkins aplenty, and maybe consider this dessert a reward for after the character sheets are put away.

JEWEL-LIKE OBJECTS OF WONDER
Teriyaki Pulled Pork Sliders with Thai Peanut Slaw

Prep Time: 1 hour | Cook Time: 8 hours, 13 minutes | Serves 12 (2 sliders apiece)

There are certain objects any hobbyist or gamer is drawn to. You see them in a fellow player's house, occupying valuable shelf space, and immediately know why they have them: true love. Perhaps it's the best figurine ever converted and painted, maybe a set of dice that utterly capture the night sky, or the limited-edition bobblehead of your favorite character that your friend has somehow gotten their hands on. These tiny sandwiches, combining the tangy zip of teriyaki and the earthy sweetness of peanut butter, are those objects—but as a food. When you plate them up, your players will immediately be drawn to them. They'll eat them incredibly fast, too, so save a few for yourself.

For Pulled Pork
¼ cup plus 2 tablespoons vegetable or
    canola oil, divided
2 (1-pound) pork tenderloins, fat trimmed
½ cup rice vinegar
¾ cup water, divided
⅓ cup soy sauce
¼ cup amber honey
1 tablespoon packed dark brown sugar
2 tablespoons minced fresh ginger
4 garlic cloves, peeled and finely
    minced or smashed
2 tablespoons cornstarch
¼ cup water
24 mini Hawaiian bread rolls, halved

For Slaw
2 cups shredded red cabbage
2 cups shredded green cabbage
2 medium carrots, peeled and grated
1 cup broccoli slaw or chopped broccoli stems
1 cup finely chopped fresh cilantro
½ cup finely chopped fresh parsley
1 medium bunch green onions, sliced thin
    (including ⅓ whites of each stem)
¼ cup olive oil
¼ cup rice vinegar
1 tablespoon soy sauce
¼ cup creamy peanut butter
1 clove garlic, peeled and finely
    minced or smashed
1 tablespoon minced fresh ginger
½ teaspoon salt
¼ teaspoon red pepper flakes

1. To make Pulled Pork: In a medium skillet, heat 2 tablespoons vegetable or canola oil over medium heat, then sear pork tenderloins on all sides until a brown crust develops, about 4–5 minutes per side.

2. In a slow cooker, whisk together vinegar, water, soy sauce, honey, brown sugar, remaining ¼ cup oil, ginger, and garlic. Add pork and turn to coat in sauce.

3. Cook on low 6-8 hours until pork is very tender and falls apart when pulled with a fork.

4. Transfer pork to a cutting board and shred using two forks. Set aside.

5. Pour cooking liquid from slow cooker into a small saucepan. In a small bowl, whisk together cornstarch and water, then add to cooking liquid.

6. Bring to a boil over medium heat, whisking frequently, until sauce is slightly thickened, 7–8 minutes.

7. Return pork with liquid to slow cooker to keep warm until ready to serve.

8. To make Slaw: In a large bowl, combine red and green cabbage, carrot, broccoli slaw, cilantro, parsley, and green onions.

9. In a separate small bowl, combine olive oil, vinegar, soy sauce, peanut butter, garlic, ginger, salt, and red pepper flakes.

10. Pour dressing over Slaw and toss to combine. Chill until ready to serve, at least 30 minutes.

11. Divide Pulled Pork evenly on bottom halves of bread rolls, heap with Slaw, and top with top halves of rolls. Serve on large platter.

JEWEL-LIKE WARNING

No matter how beautiful or detailed your individual sliders come out, please restrain yourself from attempting to prime and paint them. Honestly, they'll go bad before the meta makes them viable on the table again anyway.

ADAMANTINE BARS
Cherry Cheesecake Bars

Prep Time: 25 minutes | Cook Time: 35 minutes | Serves 12

Since actual adamantine bars would weigh several pounds and crack the teeth of anything but a rust monster, in this recipe we've decided to focus on their value rather than their physical qualities. A delectable brown sugar and almond crust rests beneath a cheesecake blend riddled with cherry preserves—truly a treat as magical as the most arcane of materials.

6 tablespoons cold unsalted butter
½ cup packed light brown sugar
1 cup all-purpose flour
¾ cup chopped toasted almonds
1 cup cherry preserves
1 (8-ounce) package room-temperature
 cream cheese

½ cup granulated sugar
1 large egg
2 tablespoons whole milk
½ teaspoon almond extract

1. Preheat oven to 350°F and grease an 8" square baking pan with nonstick cooking spray.

2. In a large bowl, cream butter and brown sugar together. Mix in flour and almonds until mixture reaches a crumbly consistency. Reserve ½ cup crumb mixture and press remaining mixture into prepared baking pan.

3. Bake 12–15 minutes until crust is golden. Remove from oven and cool 5 minutes (maintain the oven temperature).

4. Spread preserves over cooled crust.

5. In a medium bowl, cream together cream cheese and granulated sugar. Blend in egg, milk, and almond extract. Spread over preserves, then sprinkle with remaining crumb mixture.

continued on next page

6. Bake for 20 minutes. Remove from oven and cool completely in pan, about 30 minutes, before cutting. Serve immediately or chilled.

STUCK IN THE MITHRIL WITH YOU

Looking to proffer the whole gamut of magical metals? Luckily, these treats are versatile and couldn't be easier to modify with one quick substitution: those preserves. Swap in blueberry for cherry, and you've got Electrum Bars. Throw in some apricot preserves, and you've made mithril. Jalapeño preserves? Sure. Just tell everyone in attendance that they're Abyssal Blood Iron or something similarly imposing.

CAULDRON OF JOYS
Pork Belly Rillons

Prep Time: 1 hour | Cook Time: 1 hour, 30 minutes | Serves 16

If you need to captivate a crowd, you can't do much better than a simmering cauldron of tender, rich, sweet pork simmered in wine and sugar until it's essentially candy. You'll be sure to see an immediate modifier to everyone's reactions when these delectable bursts of magical flavor hit the table. Serve with mashed potatoes and a light salad, or dirty rice and summery beer, and you'll be the enchanter of your evening, every time.

2 pounds skinless pork belly, cut into 1" cubes
1 tablespoon kosher salt
2 cups granulated sugar

1 (25-ounce) bottle full-bodied red wine
1 small sprig fresh rosemary
1 small bunch fresh thyme

1. In a large bowl, toss pork cubes in salt to cover.

2. In a small saucepan, combine sugar and wine and simmer over low heat to thicken and reduce by roughly half, about 15–30 minutes.

3. Add pork to a Dutch oven and pour wine mixture over pork. Top with herbs.

4. Cover and simmer over low heat 1 hour until pork fat is rendered soft.

5. Place rillons on a wire rack over a parchment paper–lined baking sheet to cool 15 minutes. Remove herbs before serving.

> **CAULDRON MAINTENANCE**
>
> As with any other high-end magical device, you should exercise great care when using your cauldron, or you could unleash horrors that will destroy your adventuring party, your sanity, and, more relevantly, your kitchen. In this case, vigilantly watch your bubbling pot of pork delight to ensure it doesn't boil over, as the syrupy contents therein will crust over anything in sight.

COPPER PIECES
Salted Caramel Lace Cookies

Prep Time: 12 minutes | Cook Time: 14 minutes | Serves 9

You might be wondering what something so humble and utterly mundane as the copper piece is doing here among these many wonders arcane. It's simple, really; the copper piece is unique in how gleefully it can be disposed of. When placed on a table, these crisp, lacy cookies, rich with caramel flavor, will vanish at the same speed as money from a slain dragon's hoard. Double or triple this recipe as needed, because everyone loves it when the table loot goes Monty Haul.

½ cup cold unsalted butter
⅔ cup packed light brown sugar
¼ teaspoon ground cinnamon
¼ teaspoon salt

¾ cup almond flour
1 tablespoon light corn syrup
¼ teaspoon flaked sea salt

1. Preheat oven to 350°F and line a baking sheet with parchment paper.

2. In a medium saucepan, melt butter over medium heat (3–5 minutes).

3. In a large bowl, combine brown sugar, cinnamon, salt, and flour.

4. Once butter has fully melted, add corn syrup to saucepan, then whisk in brown sugar mixture. Stir continuously for about 2 minutes until sugar partially dissolves. Remove saucepan from heat.

5. Scoop small teaspoons of batter onto prepared baking sheet, separating by about 2"–3".

6. Bake until edges turn golden brown and centers completely spread, about 6–7 minutes. Watch cookies carefully while baking to avoid burning.

continued on next page

7. Remove from oven and slide parchment paper with cookies from baking sheet onto a wire rack. Sprinkle cookies with sea salt and cool 10 minutes before serving.

CONVERSION RATES

Should you plan to take these to a potluck or other food sharing occasion, make sure you're coming away with your money's worth. Ten of these cookies are worth one silver piece, rated here for convenience as at least two slices of pepperoni pizza. One hundred will net you a gold coin, or, in the parlance of food conversions, three full sleeves of Oreo cookies brought by that lazy guy who always brings Oreos.

REMARKABLY MOVABLE RODS
Candied Bacon

Prep Time: 15 minutes | Cook Time: 30 minutes | Serves 12

We'll admit it, we're over the Immovable Rod. It's versatile, sure, but it's played out. So set it aside and try out these delightful strips of caramelized, nutty bacon. They tend to move exceptionally fast and will never remain where you left them, but the difference in edibility is remarkable. Please note that oven-baked bacon doesn't crisp much when cooling, so let these cook to your preferred level of crisp before removing to cool.

½ cup packed light brown sugar
½ cup chopped pecans or walnuts
¼ teaspoon cayenne pepper

½ pound thick-cut bacon, cut in
 half crosswise
2 tablespoons maple syrup

1. Preheat oven to 400°F. Line a baking sheet with aluminum foil and place a wire rack on top.

2. In the bowl of a food processor, add brown sugar and nuts and pulse until nuts are finely chopped. Add cayenne and pulse to combine.

3. Place bacon on wire rack, ensuring strips do not touch. Bake 5 minutes.

4. Remove bacon from oven and sprinkle brown sugar mixture over each strips. Drizzle with maple syrup.

5. Return to oven and bake 20–25 minutes until bacon has reached your preferred level of crispness, checking occasionally to prevent burning.

6. Cool completely, about 30 minutes, before serving.

> **HEAT OF THE MOMENT**
> If you have a vulnerability to heat, you may find yourself viewing this ingredient list with some trepidation. Fear not! The cayenne is there to provide a necessary balance that keeps this mystical meat candy zippy and balanced. That said, if you are dedicated in your avoidance of the hotter spices, you can always substitute an equivalent amount of dry mustard, which will produce similar results with less heat.

ICY BURST BANANAS
Frozen Banana Yogurt Pops

Prep Time: 3 hours | Cook Time: N/A | Serves 8

A skilled enchanter can imbue virtually any weapon with magical fury, whether it be the finest work of the mountain smiths or a pitted blade stolen from a kobold warren. It takes a truly skilled enchanter, however, to enchant a banana. Instead, dip them in yogurt, roll them in cereal, and set them aside until your party needs a victory celebration. Careful though—on a critical hit, these will inflict brain freeze (save ends).

¾ cup vanilla or chocolate yogurt
2 cups Cocoa Pebbles or Fruity
  Pebbles cereal

8 craft sticks
4 medium ripe bananas, peeled
  and cut in half crosswise

1. In a small bowl, add yogurt. In a separate small bowl, add cereal.

2. Insert craft sticks into the cut side of bananas.

3. Dip bananas in yogurt, rolling to ensure full coverage, then roll in cereal to coat.

4. Transfer finished bananas to a baking sheet lined with wax paper, then place in freezer.

5. Freeze until fully firm, about 1–2 hours. Serve immediately or store bananas in airtight containers and return to freezer until ready to serve.

THE TRAPPINGS OF ENCHANTMENT

Wizards hate to admit it, but the vast majority of spell components and magical special effects are just window dressing, easily substituted to impress a new crowd. In that spirit, when creating your Icy Burst Bananas, you should feel empowered to experiment. Try fruity yogurts and cereals, or abandon cereals entirely for various nuts. You'll still end up with a cold-infused mallet of remarkable flavor.

Chapter 5

FINGER FIENDS:
DAINTIES FOR DEMONS AND FRIENDS

Within this chapter you'll find a motley assemblage of dungeon underdogs eager to prove something: goblinoids, lesser undead, all the foes that harry a party with numbers and cleverness instead of their sheer might. As a green recruit to the adventuring world, these are the sort of enemies you'll encounter, the stepping-stones to greatness. Though they may not be especially imposing in battle, they make for a fantastic feast in food format, so get cooking and dig in. Remember, never neglect the little guys!

CLOAKERS
Scallion Pancakes

Prep Time: 1 hour, 45 minutes | **Cook Time: 35 minutes** | **Serves 12**

Hiding in plain sight, the cloaker utilizes a cunning camouflage spell to pretend to be a simple pancake or flatbread, drawing in unsuspecting adventurers who are unprepared for an ambush of zingy green onions, warm sesame, and the heat of red pepper in every bite. Cloakers pair well with a great deal of dips, but a voluminous cloak of Hoisin Dip will further obscure their details in delicious shadows, increasing the terror and flavor.

For Pancakes
3 tablespoons sesame seeds
2 tablespoons sesame oil
2 cups unbleached all-purpose flour
1 tablespoon cornstarch
1 large egg
6 medium green onions, sliced, divided
½ teaspoon kosher salt
2 cups water
4 tablespoons peanut oil
1 teaspoon red pepper flakes

For Hoisin Dip
¼ cup soy sauce
2 tablespoons hoisin sauce
1 tablespoon water
1 clove garlic, peeled and minced
1 teaspoon chopped fresh green onion
½ teaspoon sesame oil
½ teaspoon granulated sugar
¼ teaspoon crushed or minced fresh ginger

1. To make Pancakes: In a small frying pan, toast sesame seeds over medium heat until golden brown, about 3 minutes. Remove seeds from heat and transfer to a small bowl. Add sesame oil and mix.

2. In a large bowl, combine flour, cornstarch, egg, ⅔ of green onions, salt, water, and sesame seed mixture.

3. In a large frying pan, heat 2 tablespoons peanut oil over medium-high heat. Spoon batter into pan in 3" circles. Cook 1–4 spoonfuls at a time, depending on size of pan, until golden brown and crisp, about 3 minutes per side. Transfer to a large serving plate and repeat with remaining batter, adding more peanut oil to pan as needed to prevent sticking.

continued on next page

4. Garnish with remaining ⅓ of green onions.

5. To make Hoisin Dip: Combine all ingredients in a small bowl. Cover and refrigerate 1 hour or up to overnight.

6. Pour Hoisin Dip into a small saucepan and heat over medium heat 5 minutes. Serve warm alongside Scallion Pancakes.

CAMOUFLAGED CREATIONS

Cloakers are but one of a vast swathe of dungeon creatures that rely on the art of looking like something else to survive in dungeons. If you wish to prepare a feast that no one will see coming until it's far too late, consider inspiration from others of this sort. A living wall of meatloaf, perhaps, or our own Mimic Munchies (see recipe in this chapter). For best results, insist that all of the food you are serving are cloaks and treasure chests, to the point that your friends try to commit you. That's role-playing!

BUGBEAR-Y CRUMBLES
Berry Crumble Cups

Prep Time: 20 minutes | Cook Time: 35 minutes | Serves 6

Of all the goblinoids, bugbears tend to be the least understood. Unlike their smaller brethren, they're enormous, hairy beasts covered in a thick integument of fur. This fur can even render a bugbear "cute" with a certain mindset and a bit of distance, but unlike these delightful ramekins of sweet berry blend and warm crumble crust, bugbears become decidedly not cute at the same alarming speed with which they close that distance.

½ cup all-purpose flour
½ cup packed light brown sugar
¾ cup granulated sugar, divided
½ teaspoon ground cinnamon
⅛ teaspoon salt

½ cup rolled oats
6 tablespoons cold salted butter, cut
 into small pieces
4 cups frozen mixed berries
2 tablespoons cornstarch

1. Preheat oven to 350°F.

2. In a large bowl, use a fork to combine flour, brown sugar, ¼ cup granulated sugar, cinnamon, salt, and oats. Add butter in batches, using fork to cut butter into flour and sugar until the mixture resembles crumbly wet sand. Place in refrigerator to chill until ready to use.

3. In a separate large bowl, combine berries, remaining ½ cup granulated sugar, and cornstarch until berries are coated evenly. Divide between six 6-ounce ramekins. Top with chilled crumble topping.

4. Bake until top is golden and fruit is bubbly, about 35 minutes. Remove from oven and let sit at least 10 minutes before serving.

ORIGIN OF THE SPECIES

The term "bugbear" most likely derives from the Middle English word *Bugge*, meaning "a frightening thing," or the Old Welsh term *Bwg*, which means "evil spirit." If you want to create an especially bwg-y crumble, we recommend substituting local berries for the blend. Blackberries, bilberries, and especially cowberries (you'll most likely recognize them by the name "lingonberry") can make a tasty dessert here.

CARNIVOROUS PLANTS
Thai Larb Salad

Prep Time: 20 minutes | Cook Time: 8 minutes | Serves 4

In a dangerous world of dungeon adventure, it's difficult to be certain that there's really anything that won't try to eat you eventually, including but not limited to trees, flowers, some bushes, vines, and mushrooms. That last one isn't a plant; we just want you to be careful out there. While re-creating a giant hypercarnivorous vine is difficult, and eating real-world carnivorous plants is unrealistic, a sensible solution would be these incredible spiced lettuce wraps, heaped high with ground meat ready for immediate digestion. Just eat them before they eat you.

1 tablespoon uncooked long-grain white rice
1 tablespoon vegetable oil
4 cloves garlic, peeled and thinly sliced
1 tablespoon plus 1 teaspoon granulated
 sugar, divided
½ pound ground pork or beef
2 tablespoons plus 1 teaspoon Asian
 fish sauce, divided
⅛ teaspoon salt
⅛ teaspoon ground black pepper

¼ small red onion, peeled and thinly sliced
¼ cup torn fresh mint leaves
¼ cup torn fresh Thai basil leaves
3 Thai chilies, seeded and thinly sliced,
 divided
¼ cup roughly chopped fresh
 cilantro leaves
2 tablespoons fresh lime juice
1 tablespoon water
8 large Boston lettuce leaves

1. In a medium skillet, toast rice over medium heat, shaking the pan regularly to prevent burning, until the rice is browned, about 3 minutes. Transfer rice to a small plate to cool completely, about 10 minutes.

2. In a spice grinder or food processor, grind cooled rice to a powder. Set aside.

3. Add oil to skillet used for rice over medium-low heat. Add garlic and cook 1 minute or until golden brown. Add 1 teaspoon sugar, gently incorporate, and cook 20 seconds.

4. Add pork and increase heat to medium-high, using a spatula or spoon to break up meat until finely crumbled. Cook 3 minutes or until

continued on next page

no pink remains. Add 1 teaspoon fish sauce and season with salt and pepper, then remove from heat.

5. Stir in onion, mint, basil, ⅓ of chilies, and cilantro. Sprinkle rice powder over pork mixture, then transfer mixture to a large bowl.

6. In a small bowl, combine lime juice, remaining 2 tablespoons fish sauce, remaining 1 tablespoon sugar, remaining ⅔ of chilies, and water until sugar is completely dissolved.

7. On a serving platter, arrange lettuce leaves around dipping sauce. Serve alongside pork. (Alternatively, pork can be served on lettuce leaves.)

A VORACIOUS APPROXIMATION

Obviously, attempting to re-create carnivorous flora for consumption requires some thoughtful substitutions, since, of course, creeper vines that drag you into a cave aren't real, and actual carnivorous plants are tiny. Have you ever seen a Venus flytrap in person? There's a reason they aren't called Venus hobbit traps.

CORN OFF THE KOB-OLD
Elote Bowls

Prep Time: 30 minutes | Cook Time: 8 minutes | Serves 6

We promise, this is the last kobold pun...even though, unlike a non-ambush kobold encounter, that won't be easy! If you've never tried Mexican-style street corn, you're in for a delight. Freshly griddled corn rubbed down with the slightly acidic tang of mayonnaise and crema, topped with rich, salty Cotija cheese and brought to spicy life with chili powder, this BBQ staple elevates corn to the similar vaunted status in which kobolds hold dragons. We've omitted the corn cobs in this recipe, creating a shareable, scoopable bowl and saving our tiny yapping friends the indignity of a cob half their own size slowing them down.

6 medium ears corn, husked
¼ cup mayonnaise
¼ cup sour cream or Mexican crema
¾ cup crumbled Cotija cheese, divided

¾ teaspoon ancho chili powder, divided
1 clove garlic, peeled and minced
¼ cup finely chopped fresh cilantro
1 medium lime, cut into wedges

1. Preheat grill to medium-high heat.

2. Grill corn, turning frequently on all sides, until kernels start to char, 5–8 minutes. Once all the cobs are grilled, allow them to cool slightly, about 3 minutes, then cut off all kernels, placing in a medium bowl.

3. Add mayonnaise, sour cream or crema, ½ cup Cotija, ½ teaspoon chili powder, garlic, and cilantro to bowl and toss until corn is fully coated.

4. Pour corn mixture into six serving dishes and sprinkle with remaining ¼ cup cheese and remaining ¼ teaspoon chili powder. Serve immediately with lime wedges.

PAYING HOMAGE TO DRAGONS

If you want to amp up the flavors of this dish, you can toss in some pickled or roasted jalapeño to bring an extra layer of heat and acidity to the corn. Go big! Those ko-Bold flavors will...well, shoot, and here we promised not to do any more kobold puns. Look, we're as disappointed as you are.

MIMIC MUNCHIES
Decorated Chocolate Chip Cookies

Prep Time: 1 hour, 1 minutes | Cook Time: 32 minutes | Yields 8 cookies

Mimics are deadly dungeon ambush predators, capable of near-perfectly disguising themselves as any number of mundane items you might find wandering through a cavern or abandoned keep. Here we find them shaped like an easy-to-bake and surprisingly delicious chocolate chip cookie, a sure crowd-eater...I mean, pleaser. Crowd-pleaser.

¾ cup room-temperature unsalted butter
1 cup packed light brown sugar
½ cup granulated sugar
1 large egg plus 1 large egg yolk
2 teaspoons vanilla extract
2⅛ cups all-purpose flour
½ teaspoon salt

½ teaspoon baking soda
12 ounces semisweet chocolate chips
32 jumbo candy eyes
1 (16-ounce) container chocolate frosting
8 cherry Airheads, cut in half
48 mini marshmallows, cut into
  pointed teeth

1. In the bowl of a stand mixer, cream butter, brown sugar, and granulated sugar on medium speed 1 minute or until well blended. Slowly add egg, egg yolk, and vanilla and continue to cream until fully incorporated.

2. In a medium bowl, combine flour, salt, and baking soda, then slowly stir into wet ingredients before removing bowl from stand mixer.

3. Use a wooden spoon or spatula to fold chocolate chips into batter.

4. Scoop dough into sixteen cookies (about ¼ cup dough per cookie). Place cookies on two parchment paper–lined baking sheets at least 1" apart, then refrigerate 1 hour. With 15 minutes of refrigeration remaining, preheat oven to 350°F.

5. Bake cookies one baking sheet at a time on center rack 12–16 minutes each (checking occasionally after 12 minutes) until cookies begin to crisp around the edges. Remove from oven.

continued on next page

6. Cool cookies completely on a wire rack, at least 30 minutes.

7. Spoon a small amount of chocolate frosting on the bottom of one cookie, and put another cookie on top to create a sandwich. Repeat with remaining cookies to create 8 sandwiches total.

8. Attach 2 candy eyes to top of each cookie using chocolate frosting. Place half of an Airhead coming out of each mouth to create an evil, lolling tongue. Use more frosting to attach six marshmallow "teeth" to each top cookie, above the tongue. Serve immediately.

TREASURE TELLS

Personally, we aren't sure how easy it is for mimics to go around fooling all these highly trained adventurers. Don't they spot the huge googly eyes and lolling giant tongues? As adventurers, we'd just avoid any treasure chest that looks like a Tex Avery character mid-catcall, but what do we know—we're not paladins.

MY MY MYCONIDS
Italian Stuffed Mushrooms

Prep Time: 20 minutes | Cook Time: 23 minutes | Serves 18

Skulking about in caves, the myconids will eat you if you'll let them, so why not return the favor! These tiny caps make the perfect party starter.

3 tablespoons room-temperature salted
 butter, divided

⅓ cup finely chopped mushroom stems

3 (about ¼ cup) medium green onions,
 chopped

¼ cup seeded and chopped red bell pepper

1½ cups breadcrumbs

2 teaspoons Italian seasoning

¼ teaspoon salt

¼ teaspoon ground black pepper

36 (about 1 pound) medium white
 mushroom caps

¼ cup grated Parmesan cheese

1. Preheat oven to 350°F.

2. In a large skillet, melt 2 tablespoons butter over medium-high heat (about 2–3 minutes). Cook mushroom stems, green onions, and bell pepper 3 minutes, stirring frequently, until onions are soft. Remove from heat and transfer to a medium bowl. Stir in breadcrumbs, Italian seasoning, salt, and pepper.

3. Fill each mushroom cap with one heaping scoop of breadcrumb mixture.

4. In a small microwave-safe bowl, melt remaining 1 tablespoon butter in microwave (about 20–30 seconds), then spread out in a 13" × 9" baking dish. Place mushroom caps in dish. Sprinkle with Parmesan and bake 15 minutes. Remove from oven.

5. Turn oven to high broil and cook mushrooms 3"–4" from heat about 2 minutes or until tops are light brown, then serve immediately.

BUT I'M A FUNGI

These aren't made out of actual sentient myconid folk. Instead, they're crafted from the myconid's non-sentient young during the part of their life cycle where they're still sessile and adorable little fungus critters.

ZOMBEAN ATTACK
Black Bean Antojitos

Prep Time: 15 minutes | Cook Time: 10 minutes | Serves 4

Mindless, unstoppable, and eager to devour anything that stands in their way, your players will often be starving after a few hours of nonstop table action. With quick thinking and even faster meal preparation, you can save your friends and yourself and turn back the tide of their voracious charge with these delicious black bean and cheese rolls.

3 medium red bell peppers

1 (16-ounce) can black beans, drained and rinsed

2 cloves garlic, peeled and minced

2 tablespoons lime juice

1 teaspoon ground cumin

1 teaspoon ground coriander

¼ teaspoon salt

¼ teaspoon ground black pepper

8 (6") whole-wheat flour tortillas

1 medium avocado, peeled, pitted, and sliced

1 cup shredded Cheddar cheese

1. Place bell peppers on a parchment paper–lined baking sheet and broil on high heat 5–10 minutes, turning often as the skin turns black and blisters. When blackening is mostly complete around all peppers, remove from heat and use tongs to transfer peppers to a large paper bag to cool, about 10 minutes.

2. Once cool, remove and discard blackened skin, then remove stems, seeds, and pith. Chop peppers into strips and set aside.

3. In a large bowl, mash beans and garlic with a potato masher or fork. Add lime juice, cumin, coriander, salt, and pepper and mix to combine.

4. Spread mashed bean mixture evenly over each tortilla, then divide roasted red peppers, avocado, and cheese evenly over bean mixture.

5. Roll each tortilla tightly, then cover in plastic wrap and refrigerate at least 10 minutes, up to overnight.

6. Cut each roll into 1" pieces and spear with a toothpick before serving.

TRY THE WIGHT SAUCE

These little rolls are perfectly paired with our zesty, sweet peach salsa, Critical Dip (see recipe in Chapter 3).

SKEWERED KUO-TOA
Swordfish Spiedini

Prep Time: 15 minutes | Cook Time: 9 minutes | Serves 6

Fishlike denizens of the deep reaches of the ocean and the dripping depths of oppressive cave networks throughout the world, the kuo-toa are fierce hunters and masters of the trident. We've attempted here to honor their ecology by flame-roasting a fierce hunter fish and serving it up skewered on a pike. Strands of rich bacon wind throughout, suggesting the kelp forests in which...just kidding, that doesn't really track. It's just there because bacon is delicious.

2 tablespoons extra-virgin olive oil
1 teaspoon herbes de Provence
½ teaspoon salt
½ teaspoon ground black pepper

1½ pounds skinless swordfish steak, cut into 1" cubes
6 strips regular-cut bacon

1. Preheat grill to high heat.

2. In a medium bowl, combine oil, herbes de Provence, salt, and pepper. Add swordfish cubes and toss to coat.

3. Thread ⅙ of swordfish cubes and 1 strip bacon onto each of six skewers, winding bacon around fish at each step.

4. Grill each skewer, turning occasionally, about 8–9 minutes until swordfish is cooked through. Serve immediately.

SAHUAGIN SURPRISE?

Kuo-toa letting you down? Well, don't you fret, because they're not the only horrifying fish in the deadly lightless reaches. You can try nearly any number of firm-fleshed fish when making this recipe, though we are partial to mako or thresher shark. Escolar is another excellent substitute. Just avoid actual sahuagin or kuo-toa, as they are notoriously difficult to ethically source and aren't safe for pregnant women or anyone else who would like to be alive.

INFERNAL'D CRAB
Deviled Crab

Prep Time: 20 minutes | Cook Time: 30 minutes | Serves 6

A fun trick in dungeon ecology is that you can affix dire or infernal templates to anything, increasing their difficulty at a terrifying pace. A dire crab may be covered from stem to stern in vicious spikes, while an infernal'd crab is broken down, mixed with cayenne and lemon, and baked with a breadcrumb topping for a crunchy texture before being served alongside crusty bread. Oh, and we suppose it breathes darkness or something.

¼ cup mayonnaise

2 tablespoons yellow mustard

1 tablespoon ketchup

1 tablespoon lemon juice

¼ teaspoon cayenne pepper

1 pound lump crabmeat, drained and shredded

½ cup seeded and finely diced red bell pepper

½ cup peeled and finely diced red onion

¼ cup panko breadcrumbs

2 teaspoons canola oil

1. Preheat oven to 425°F.

2. In a large bowl, combine mayonnaise, mustard, ketchup, lemon juice, and cayenne.

3. Add crab, bell pepper, and onion and fold until evenly mixed. Transfer mixture to a small baking dish and place on a rimmed baking sheet.

4. In a small bowl, combine breadcrumbs and oil. Sprinkle over crab mixture.

5. Bake 30 minutes or until crust is golden brown. Serve hot.

DIRE CRABBY PATTIES

To scale this beastly meal down to a more manageable sandwich, you can get it to hold together by increasing the breadcrumbs to ½ cup and adding them to the crab mixture along with a large egg. Form the mixture into patties and bake on a parchment paper–lined baking sheet. They'll make excellent—if spiky and predatory—sandwiches.

MINOTAUR CAVIAR
Cowboy Caviar

Prep Time: 1 hour, 10 minutes | **Cook Time: N/A** | **Serves 12**

We know what you're thinking: How is this not a beef recipe? They're cow people. Well, yes, but that'd be pretty heartless, right? Why not celebrate the positive aspects of minotaur culture, such as their nobility, love of mazes and maze iconography, and enjoyment of delicious avocado dips. Either serve this one as a dip with chips or spoon it over salads to add richness and flavor.

1 (15-ounce) can black beans, drained and rinsed

1 (15-ounce) can corn, drained and rinsed or 1½ cups fresh corn

3 Roma tomatoes, diced

2 medium avocados, peeled, pitted, and diced

¼ cup peeled and diced red onion

¼ cup finely chopped fresh cilantro

Juice of 1 medium lime

½ teaspoon salt

½ cup Italian dressing

1. In a large bowl, combine beans, corn, tomatoes, avocados, onion, and cilantro. Squeeze lime juice over top, then add salt and Italian dressing and stir until well combined.

2. Cover bowl and refrigerate 1 hour before serving.

BUT HOW IS IT CAVIAR?

We get it: You're wondering how we can justify calling a recipe named after the clearly mammalian minotaur a caviar, but just like you aren't sure whether the noble bull folk enjoy rich avocado dips, you similarly can't be 100 percent assured that we're lying when we claim that minotaurs are monotremes, closely related to the platypus and echidna, and lay eggs while remaining mammals. It's true! Just don't check anywhere else.

Chapter 6

THE MASSIVE MENU: BITES FOR BEHEMOUTHS

Think big with our collection of table-smashing recipes built around the thundering giants of RPGs. Games love big creatures as the centerpiece of a dungeon; there's just something cinematic and inspiring about teaming up to tear down a colossus before it flattens the nearby villages, and these plates will all take teamwork to conquer too. Giants, dragons, gods, and monsters all deconstructed into easy meals that'll feed an army, or just a game night.

DRAGON TALONS
Koobideh Skewers

Prep Time: 20 minutes | Cook Time: 16 minutes | Serves 5

Massive, preternaturally powerful, and possessed of incredible intellect that adventurers cannot begin to fathom, dragons are a terrible and awesome presence in the world. So much so, in fact, that eating dragon or even naming foods after dragons is considered in poor taste at best and dangerous in reality, as no chef wants to explain their joke to a pair of angry eyes larger than they are. One exception are these delicious meat skewers, historically grilled on sabers reminiscent of the dragon's massive claws. Redolent of garlic and onion, delicious and imposing, Dragon Talons are thought to be excused from fiery wrath solely because dragons like them too.

2 teaspoons water

4 strands saffron

½ large white onion, peeled and finely grated

1 pound ground beef

1 teaspoon salt

¼ teaspoon ground black pepper

1½ teaspoons dried sumac

1 large egg

¼ teaspoon ground turmeric

1 teaspoon crushed garlic

1. In a small microwave-safe dish, microwave water 30 seconds on high. Add saffron and allow to steep 5 minutes. Strain out stands and set saffron water aside.

2. Place onion in a cheesecloth or several paper towels and squeeze out as much liquid as possible.

3. In a large bowl, combine all remaining ingredients including saffron water. Cover and refrigerate at least 1 hour, up to overnight.

4. Preheat oven to low broil.

5. Divide meat mixture into five equal sections. Roll each section into a cylinder shape, then slide onto a flat skewer and press down on meat slightly, using wet hands to prevent sticking.

continued on next page

6. Using the flat side of a butter knife, add indentations about 1" apart along length of the meat on each skewer.

7. Place skewers on a wire rack set on a baking sheet. Broil 8 minutes, then flip skewers and broil an additional 8 minutes.

8. Remove from oven and serve skewers hot.

DRACONIC ATTENDANTS

A puissant and mighty dragon never rests in his lair unattended. Sycophantic kobolds, goblinoid mercenaries, sorcerous hangers-on of unknown provenance, and worse yet. Talons meanwhile should be served with heaped rice and cucumber salad, truer guardians than which no Talon could ask for.

ROAST PORCUS
Garlic-Studded Pork Tenderloin

Prep Time: 40 minutes | Cook Time: 40 minutes | Serves 4

When dark summoning rituals go uninterrupted by the heroes, cracks in the tenuous barrier between their world and ours grow wide enough that the mightiest overlords of the many-layered hells stalk forth...bearing main courses. Stuffed with fresh garlic and seared to lock in the flavor, this tenderloin is a meal fit to serve a king of hell...or your friends.

1 (1-pound) pork tenderloin, fat trimmed
  and silverskin removed
4 cloves garlic, peeled and slivered
¼ teaspoon salt

¼ teaspoon ground black pepper
½ teaspoon dried thyme
½ teaspoon dried rosemary
1 tablespoon canola or vegetable oil

1. Preheat oven to 400°F. Line a baking sheet with aluminum foil.

2. Using a small sharp knife, make ½"-deep cuts widthwise across the surface of entire tenderloin. Insert a sliver of garlic into each cut.

3. In a small bowl, combine salt, pepper, thyme, and rosemary. Rub spice mixture over tenderloin.

4. In a large frying pan, add oil and cook tenderloin over medium-high heat until browned, about 5 minutes per side.

5. Transfer browned tenderloin to prepared baking sheet and cook in oven until internal temperature at thickest point registers 145°F, about 18–20 minutes.

6. Remove from oven and allow to rest 10 minutes before slicing and serving.

THE 666 LAYERS OF THE SANDWICH ABYSS

One great benefit to this tenderloin is leftovers. As good cold as it is warm, once sliced fairly thin this demonic delight will make a sandwich you'll never forget. Try it with giardiniera, roasted red peppers, smoked provolone, or any other toppings you like, piled high on a ciabatta or even sourdough.

GORGON GRINDERS
Steak and Gorgonzola Sandwiches

Prep Time: 20 minutes | Cook Time: 16 minutes | Serves 4

In virtually any other circumstance, this recipe would be full of jokes about how the steak is more tender than stone, don't look a gift sandwich in the eyes, etc. But not here. Here, a gorgon is a giant metal bull that breathes noxious fumes. After some thought, a steak sandwich stuffed with roasted peppers and flavorful gorgonzola honestly seemed perfect. Plus, after eating one, we thought, "Hey, let's put the recipe in this book too."

1 (1-pound) sirloin steak
⅛ teaspoon salt
⅛ teaspoon ground black pepper

1 cup drained roasted red peppers
4 hoagie rolls, halved
½ cup crumbled gorgonzola cheese

1. Preheat grill to medium-high heat. Sprinkle both sides of steak with salt and pepper.

2. Grill steak 6–8 minutes per side to desired doneness. Remove from grill and let rest 10 minutes.

3. Slice steak against the grain into thin slices, around ⅛"–¼" thick.

4. Layer ¼ cup red peppers on bottom of each roll. Top with 2 tablespoons gorgonzola per roll. Divide steak evenly among rolls. Top with remaining half of roll. Serve immediately.

BULL'S STRENGTH

Fine, we're aware that some of you simply don't have the taste for the veinier cheeses. This sandwich is meant to be honoring a steel-banded cow that breathes poison farts, but it's okay—this sandwich would also be amazing with some smoked provolone.

PURPLE WORM CROSS SECTION
Ube Cake with Ube Halaya Frosting

Prep Time: 55 minutes | Cook Time: 35 minutes | Serves 8

Actually, including a recipe for roast purple worm was impractical, as the only ovens that can roast them are industrial-sized furnaces owned only by mining companies and Guy Fieri. Besides, they taste like actual dirt no matter how much thyme you rub on them. Instead, we've gone for a circular cross section, rendered in chiffon cake and colored with ube, a tasty (and earthy; that's theming!) purple yam. Double the frosting recipe if you'd like this coated top to bottom, which, trust us, you do.

For Cake
2½ cups sifted cake flour
3 teaspoons baking powder
1 teaspoon salt
1 cup ube purée
¾ cup whole milk
1 teaspoon vanilla extract
½ cup light corn syrup
7 large eggs, yolks and whites separated
½ cup vegetable oil
1 teaspoon cream of tartar
1 cup granulated sugar
6 drops red food coloring
6 drops blue food coloring

For Frosting
½ cup room-temperature unsalted butter
2 cups sifted confectioners' sugar
1½ teaspoons vanilla extract
2 tablespoons whole milk
2 tablespoons ube purée
1 drop purple food coloring
3 tablespoons sweetened condensed milk

1. To make Cake: Preheat oven to 325°F. Line three 9" round cake pans with parchment paper.

2. In a medium bowl, combine flour, baking powder, and salt.

3. In a large bowl, add ube purée and slowly add whole milk, then vanilla, mixing until smooth. Mix in corn syrup, egg yolks, and oil. Stir in flour mixture and set aside.

4. Beat egg whites and cream of tartar until foamy, about 4 minutes. Slowly add granulated sugar and food coloring while beating until stiff peaks form. (For a deeper color, add a drop of purple food coloring while beating.) Add ⅓ of egg whites to cake batter, then gently but quickly fold in remaining ⅔ of egg whites, working carefully to keep as much air in egg whites as possible.

5. Divide batter evenly among prepared cake pans. Bake 30–35 minutes until tops spring back when gently pressed.

6. Cool cake layers in pans 10 minutes, then invert onto a wire rack and cool fully, about 1 hour, before frosting and layering.

7. To make Frosting: In a large bowl, using a hand mixer, the paddle attachment of a stand mixer, or a wooden spoon, cream butter until fluffy and light, about 3–4 minutes. Slowly beat in confectioners' sugar until fully incorporated, pausing when necessary to scrape down sides of bowl. Beat in vanilla until fully incorporated.

8. Pour in whole milk and beat an additional 3–4 minutes until fully incorporated.

9. Add ube purée and food coloring to buttercream mixture and mix continuously, adding condensed milk 1 tablespoon at a time until desired thickness is reached (should be thick enough to pipe).

10. Spread frosting on one cake layer and cover with second layer. Repeat with remaining cake to create third layer. Slice and serve.

WALK WITHOUT UBE, AND YOU WON'T FLAVOR THE WORM

Ube purée is often available frozen in Asian markets. If you can't find frozen, it is also available as a powder, which can be reconstituted following package directions. Once reconstituted, ube powder can be used in the same way and amount as purée. If you still can't find any, you can use actual purple worm, but you'll really need to wring out all the ichor. Use a cheesecloth.

SWEET TREANT
Yule Log Cake

Prep Time: 1 hour, 3 minutes | Cook Time: 12 minutes | Serves 8

Perhaps the only creature on the massive menu index to voluntarily contribute to the feast, the mighty arboreal forest defenders known as treants do occasionally require pruning, and their loss is our gain. Also, they're full of chocolate spiraled together with a delightful mascarpone cream cheese filling, and...who are we kidding? This is a cake recipe. An excellent one, sure, one worthy of the attention of a mighty man-tree of the deepest woods, but it's not carved off of one. For even more yule, make a second cake and cut it into smaller pieces to attach as wood knots to the main cake.

For Cake
¾ cup all-purpose flour
⅓ cup Hershey's Special Dark cocoa powder
1 teaspoon baking powder
½ teaspoon salt
4 large eggs, yolks and whites separated
¾ cup granulated sugar
5 tablespoons sour cream
4 tablespoons melted unsalted butter
1 teaspoon vanilla extract

For Filling
1¼ cups cold heavy whipping cream
¾ cup confectioners' sugar
1 teaspoon vanilla extract
⅛ teaspoon salt
8 ounces softened mascarpone cheese

For Ganache
8 ounces finely chopped semisweet
  chocolate
1 cup heavy whipping cream

1. To make Cake: Preheat oven to 350°F. Line a 17" × 12" jelly roll pan with parchment paper, making sure paper extends over sides of pan by at least 1".

2. In a medium bowl, whisk together flour, cocoa, baking powder, and salt. Set aside.

3. In a large bowl, whisk together egg yolks and granulated sugar. Add sour cream, butter, and vanilla and whisk until well combined.

4. Slowly incorporate dry ingredients into egg mixture and whisk gently until well combined, then set aside.

continued on next page

5. In a separate large bowl, use an electric mixer to whip egg whites on high speed until stiff peaks form.

6. Gently fold about ⅓ of whipped egg whites into Cake mixture, mixing carefully to keep as much air in as possible. Add remaining egg whites and fold in gently until fully combined.

7. Pour Cake batter evenly into prepared pan and bake 10–12 minutes until top of Cake springs back when touched and a toothpick inserted in center comes out clean.

8. Remove Cake from oven. Using parchment paper edges, immediately lift Cake out of pan and place it on a work surface. While Cake is still hot, using parchment paper and starting at the shorter end of Cake, slowly roll Cake up into a log shape. Set aside to cool completely, about 1 hour.

9. To make Filling: In a separate large bowl, add cream, confectioners' sugar, vanilla, and salt. Use an electric mixer to whip on high speed until soft peaks form, about 2–3 minutes.

10. Add mascarpone and whip until stiff peaks form, about 1–2 minutes.

11. Carefully unroll Cake, using a spatula to loosen any spots where parchment is sticking. Spread Filling evenly onto inner side of unrolled Cake, then roll back up without parchment paper.

12. Wrap Cake in plastic wrap with Cake's seam facing down and refrigerate 1 hour to firm up.

13. To make Ganache: Place chocolate in a medium bowl and set aside. In a small microwave-safe bowl, heat cream on high until it just begins to boil, about 90 seconds, then pour over chocolate.

14. Allow chocolate and cream to sit 3 minutes, then whisk until smooth. Set aside to cool to room temperature, about 10 minutes.

15. Using an electric mixer, whip cooled chocolate mixture on high speed until thick enough to spread and lighter in color.

16. Spread Ganache over outside of Cake, then use a fork to create bark-like lines. Refrigerate until ready to serve, at least 1 hour, up to 24 hours.

BAKE LIKE A TREE AND LEAF

One thing we omitted here for simplicity but that makes a fantastic addition to a cake like this is some garnish that implies forested settings. Candied cherries, sugared cranberries, and edible leaf decorations are all available in the cake decorating aisle of stores and can really take this from a chocolate log to a treant's severed arm. Wait, is that even a good thing?

HILL GIANT HURLERS
Caramel Popcorn Balls

Prep Time: 10 minutes | Cook Time: 16 minutes | Serves 12

Lumbering and somewhat dull-witted, hill giants are a fearsome foe, routinely carting around boulders they find in the hills to flatten their foes at range. Since recipes calling for actual boulders were shut down by our publishers, we've settled on these delectable giant popcorn balls, perfect for hurling at your friends and enemies alike.

10 cups popped popcorn
½ cup granulated sugar
1½ cups packed light brown sugar
1 cup light corn syrup

1 cup water
2 teaspoons white vinegar
½ teaspoon salt
½ cup room-temperature unsalted butter

1. In a large bowl, add popcorn and set aside. In a small bowl, add a spoonful of very cold water and set aside.

2. In a 2-quart saucepan, combine sugars, corn syrup, water, vinegar, and salt, then bring to a boil over medium-high heat, stirring frequently until boiling, about 7–10 minutes (watch carefully, as it can burn easily).

3. Once boiling, stir constantly until a small amount of mixture dropped into cold water forms a ball (hard-ball stage), about 2–3 minutes.

4. Once hard-ball stage is reached, reduce heat to low and stir in butter until melted, 2–3 minutes.

5. Pour syrup over popcorn, stirring until well coated. Cool 2 minutes.

6. Using buttered or oiled hands, shape popcorn into twelve balls. Cool completely before serving, about 15 minutes.

WHO WANTS BONE BREAD, ANYWAY?

As we workshopped recipes in the image of giants, we passed on a lot of unsavory concepts. Their food tends to be...unpalatable. Halfings squashed to jelly under-butt? Ground bone bread? Try dipping these in melted chocolate instead.

DIRE BOAR BAGELS
Meat Lover's Pizza Bagels

Prep Time: 10 minutes | Cook Time: 10 minutes | Serves 3

Snack-sized pizzas loaded with every sort of meat you can reasonably carve off a dire boar, the only problem with these savory treats is the difficulty of capturing and butchering such a titanic beast, especially with all the bony plates and their pesky lack of natural existence. For this application, we've brought in good old pork from, presumably, a not-dire pig. Hard to blame us; pork is a reasonable substitute, and it won't drive you into a feral murderous rage. Well, unless you take the DM's pizza.

3 bagels, plain or any savory variety,
  halved
½ cup pizza sauce
1 cup shredded mozzarella cheese, divided
1 (8-ounce) Spanish-style chorizo sausage,
  thinly sliced

½ cup drained roasted red peppers
3 strips regular-cut bacon, cooked
  and chopped
⅓ cup thinly sliced button mushrooms
½ small red onion, peeled and thinly sliced
⅓ cup chopped arugula

1. Preheat oven to 425°F.

2. Arrange bagel halves cut-side up on an aluminum foil–lined baking sheet. Spread a thin layer of pizza sauce over each bagel, then sprinkle about ½ cup mozzarella evenly on top. Arrange chorizo, red peppers, bacon, mushrooms, and onion on bagels, then sprinkle remaining ½ cup mozzarella on top.

3. Bake 8–10 minutes until cheese is melted and golden. Remove from oven, immediately cover bagels with arugula, and serve.

EVEN DIRER BOARS

You're probably wondering if this will work as a regular old pizza. Of course it will! You provide the dough, and this set of toppings won't steer you wrong. We're just trying to focus on bite-sized table presentation, since pizza tends to dominate the exact spot where the dungeon map would go, and who wants that?

SUMMON WALL OF GARLIC BREAD
Stuffed Garlic Loaf

Prep Time: 15 minutes | Cook Time: 25 minutes | Serves 5

Walls of flame, stone, steel, fire, salt, and even thorns are common tools in the arsenals of puissant and canny wizards. They can be dense, dangerous, and impenetrable. They can reshape a battlefield and turn the tides of a mighty army. This one...well, it tends to feed an army more than reshape it, but if anything, that just makes the wizard more popular! Summon a few of these and watch the tides of the table turn in your favor!

1 large loaf ciabatta bread
6 cloves garlic, peeled and minced
½ cup chopped fresh parsley
½ cup room-temperature salted butter, cubed

2 tablespoons olive oil
1 teaspoon salt
1 teaspoon ground black pepper
1 cup grated Parmesan cheese

1. Preheat oven to 425°F.

2. Cut thick slices into ciabatta, leaving about ½" at bottom of bread uncut.

3. In a medium bowl, combine remaining ingredients. Evenly stuff mixture into cuts in bread.

4. Wrap bread tightly in aluminum foil, place on a baking sheet, and bake 25 minutes.

5. Remove bread from foil and bake an additional 5 minutes on baking sheet to crisp up the outside. Serve warm.

SUMMON POOL OF DIPPING SAUCE

A complementary spell that serves to take the Wall of Garlic Bread to its logical peak, the Summon Pool of Dipping Sauce incantation is so easy it doesn't really require a recipe in this book, let alone a spellbook entry. The material component? A warm bowl of marinara sauce or a cool bowl of ranch dressing. The somatic component? Put it on the table near the garlic bread. The verbal component? "Mmmmm."

SMOKIN' KRAKEN
Smoked Salmon Bites

Prep Time: 20 minutes | Cook Time: N/A | Serves 14

The most terrible, imposing, and murderous monster of the deep seas (non-Mythos category), the kraken is a horrific squid-like beast that hides deep in the blackest reaches of the depths, rising to pull ships and sailors to a watery doom. We've attempted here to take a little of the fear out of the relationship by cubing the beast and serving it up on toothpicks. An eye for an eye, and a ship for a snack. By using smoked salmon, these little bites impart a hearty flavor spiked through with the delightful zing of lemon and the cool of dill. A rare opportunity to enjoy seafood before you *are* seafood.

8 ounces softened cream cheese
½ cup sour cream
½ teaspoon garlic powder
Zest of 1 large lemon
½ teaspoon salt

¼ cup chopped fresh dill
3 (9") soft flour tortillas
16 ounces smoked salmon slices
2 tablespoons softened salted butter

1. In a medium bowl, combine cream cheese, sour cream, garlic powder, lemon zest, salt, and dill.

2. Spread ½ of cream cheese mixture on 1 tortilla, then top with ½ of smoked salmon.

3. Spread butter thinly on a second tortilla. Place tortilla butter-side down onto salmon layer of first tortilla.

4. Repeat steps with remaining cream cheese mixture, salmon, butter, and tortilla.

5. Cover tortilla stack with plastic wrap, then compress with a heavy, flat object such as a frying pan or large book.

6. Refrigerate, still covered with plastic wrap, at least 4 hours, up to two days.

continued on next page

7. Using a serrated knife, trim edges to square off tortilla stack. Cut tortilla square into six or seven even strips, then cut each strip into squares. Spear each square with a toothpick and serve chilled.

SQUID PRO QUO

You may be wondering why these appetizers are made with salmon and not the theoretically more appropriate calamari or squid. Well, we have a few reasons. Squid is too chewy to pair well with sandwiching tortillas. A small bite, smoked salmon is far easier to find in stores, and, frankly, we don't want any krakens catching word we're eating their little buddies. We'd like to go surfing again someday without being messily pulled apart by man-sized suckers, after all.

MARSHMALLOW GOLEMS
Sweet Potato Casserole Bites

Prep Time: 20 minutes | Cook Time: 22 minutes | Serves 6

Sweet, a little sticky, and programmed to follow the single command you impart on paper stored in their heads, marshmallow golems are definitely a regularly appearing fantasy monster from a wide variety of games and stories and not just a monster we made up to work in a recipe we enjoyed. These roasted sweet potato coins, topped with marshmallow, syrup, and pecans, capture everything you love about Thanksgiving-style sweet potatoes in a snackable, shareable format. Build a few for your next game night and thrill as they set about guarding your stomach from encroaching hunger.

4 medium sweet potatoes, peeled and
  cut into ¼" rounds
2 tablespoons melted unsalted butter
1 teaspoon maple syrup
¼ teaspoon salt
1 (10-ounce) bag marshmallows
½ cup pecan halves

1. Preheat oven to 400°F.

2. On a large baking sheet, toss sweet potatoes with butter and maple syrup and arrange in an even layer. Season with salt.

3. Bake 20 minutes or until fork-tender. Remove baking sheet from oven.

4. Turn oven to high broil. Top each sweet potato round with a marshmallow and broil, watching carefully, until marshmallow is puffed and golden, about 1–2 minutes. Remove from oven, immediately top each marshmallow with a pecan half, and serve.

GOLEM RECONSTRUCTION

A simple serving suggestion for these delectable treats is to just place them on a tray, arranged in the shape of a hulking humanoid monster. It's fun, connects well to the theme, and allows for gameful banter over who gets to eat the head and learn the activation codes installed in this model.

Chapter 7

LUSCIOUS LOCATIONS: FARE FOR FARAWAY PLACES

From the depths of the deepest sea to the highest reaches of snow-capped mountains, adventure awaits just about anywhere a party cares to look. Why not transfer that energy to your kitchen with a selection of recipes that call up the iconic battlefields of RPG history? Got an adventure coming up that takes place someplace new and novel? Craft up a snack from this chapter to accent the terrain you're taking your party to.

TAVERN FARE
Midwestern Party Mix

Prep Time: 20 minutes | Cook Time: 30 minutes | Serves 20

Every adventure has to start somewhere, and there might as well be snacks. Something salty and spicy to keep the ales flowing is a popular find on the bars of taverns the world over, and this mix is a hearty blend of crunchy snacks, sharp garlic, and fresh rosemary that'll put everyone in the party, assembled or otherwise, in the adventuring mood. Grab a handful and see who else wants to raid the kobolds of Moonwater Keep.

3 cups pecan halves

2 cups oyster crackers

2 cups square white Cheddar cheese crackers

1½ cups grated Parmesan cheese

1 cup pumpkin seeds

2 tablespoons packed light brown sugar

2 tablespoons chopped fresh rosemary

2 teaspoons crushed red pepper

4 cloves garlic, peeled and minced

½ cup melted salted butter

1. Preheat oven to 300°F.

2. In a large bowl, combine all ingredients except butter. Drizzle in butter, then stir gently to coat.

3. Spread mixture out on a large, aluminum foil–lined rimmed baking sheet. Bake 15 minutes; toss, then bake another 15 minutes.

4. Cool 15 minutes, then serve immediately, or store at room temperature in an airtight container for up to one week.

FARE ENOUGH?

Careful, this mix goes fast, and players tend to hang around the tavern longer than the adventure module ever thinks they will. The combination means that, half the time, Tavern Fare is gone too soon, so take the hint and double the recipe.

WIZARD'S TOWER
Hot Water Crust Meat Pie

Prep Time: 24 hours | Cook Time: 2 hours, 59 minutes | Serves 8

A freestanding structure riddled with complexity, arcane detail, and ancient technique, the only thing truly separating the hot water crust Wizard's Tower from the genuine article is 50 feet of height and a wizard in there somewhere. (Though we're not going to stop you if you want to cram some wizard into yours; we've gone with the somewhat less fireball-prone chicken and pork sausage filling.) As you're constructing a home and sanctum, it's only natural that the flavors and textures are homey, reminiscent of Christmas dinner and warm nights by the fireside, studying sorcerous tomes of arcana and mysticism. Oh, and thyme.

For Crust
4 cups all-purpose flour
1 teaspoon salt
½ cup water
6 tablespoons cold unsalted butter
½ cup lard

For Filling
4 (6-ounce) boneless, skinless chicken
   breasts, diced into ½" cubes
1 pound pork sausage, casings removed
1 cup chopped pancetta or bacon
2 tablespoons chopped fresh parsley
1 tablespoon chopped fresh sage
1 teaspoon chopped fresh thyme

½ teaspoon ground mace
¼ teaspoon allspice
Zest of 1 medium lemon
½ teaspoon salt
1½ teaspoons ground black pepper
2 tablespoons cold unsalted butter

For Stock
1 (½-tablespoon) packet unflavored
   gelatin powder
¼ ounce cold water
2 cups chicken stock

For Glaze
1 large egg

1. **To make Crust:** In a large bowl, sift flour and salt, then make a well in center. Set aside.

2. In a small saucepan, cook water, butter, and lard over medium heat. Stir until butter and lard are fully melted (3–5 minutes), bring to a boil, another 5–7 minutes, then remove from heat.

continued on next page

3. Pour butter mixture into center of flour. Mix with a wooden spoon until a shaggy dough forms, then mix with oiled hands until smooth and elastic.

4. Loosely cover bowl with plastic wrap and place in a warm area to rise 20 minutes.

5. To make Filling: In a separate large bowl, combine all ingredients until well mixed. Set aside.

6. To make Stock: In a small bowl, add gelatin powder to cold water and allow to bloom, about 5 minutes.

7. While gelatin is blooming, in a medium saucepan, heat stock to a simmer over medium-low heat, about 5–7 minutes. Add bloomed gelatin and mix until gelatin is fully dissolved. Transfer to a small container and refrigerate up to 24 hours until ready to use.

8. Preheat oven to 350°F. Line an 8" round pie or cake pan with greased parchment paper, ensuring that some paper rises above edge of pan for easy pie removal.

9. Uncover Crust. Roll ⅔ of dough into a large, flat disc, and place in bottom of prepared pan. Gently mold and press dough until pastry covers the bottom and sides of pan, maintaining as even a surface as possible and using torn segments to patch any leaks or cracks.

10. Fill Crust with Filling, carefully packing in to avoid air bubbles.

11. To make Glaze: In a small bowl, beat egg until frothy.

12. Use a small pastry brush to moisten top edges of Crust around pan with some of Glaze.

13. Roll out remaining dough and cut a circle large enough to fit top of pan. Place over Filling and seal edges, then trim off any excess edge. Use a knife to cut a small hole in top center of pie, and use any remaining dough to create shingles, windows, or other desired decorations. Press decorations into pie top. Brush pie top with more Glaze.

14. Lay a sheet of aluminum foil over pie and bake 2 hours. Remove from oven and allow to rest 40 minutes, increasing oven temperature to 375°F while resting.

15. Carefully remove pie from pan by pulling excess parchment paper, then brush pie with remaining Glaze.

16. Return pie to oven without pan and continue to bake 30 minutes or until golden brown all over. If top of pie is browning too fast, cover with aluminum foil while sides brown.

17. Remove pie from oven and cool 2 hours, then cover and refrigerate overnight.

18. In a medium saucepan, reheat jellied Stock over low heat (or in a double boiler) until syrupy and fluid, about 10 minutes. Place pie on a rimmed baking sheet. Using a funnel, pour as much stock as possible into steam hole on top of pie. When pie begins to overflow, wait a minute or so, then resume pouring. Slice and serve.

EPIC LEVEL PROGRESSION

The Wizard's Tower is far and away the most complicated recipe presented within these pages. While we didn't organize the book by spell levels, this is the 9. You can learn this or Wish, essentially. We humbly recommend this one, as no one has been instructed to twist the recipe against you. You'll know immediately if it works, and we don't actually know how to cast Wish.

TRAIL RATIONS
Oven S'mores

Prep Time: 25 minutes | Cook Time: 19 minutes | Yields 12 s'mores

Originally, this was a recipe for lembas bread, the magical repast crafted with precision by the elves of the deep wood forests, but that was, among other things, trademarked and magical, and anyway it sort of tasted like plywood. So we've gone with what is certainly more delicious, if not more practical, than the waybread of the children of Fëanor: oven-baked s'mores, improved beyond the standard campfire model with the addition of buttery-smooth liquid chocolate and the careful precision of a broiler. Once you hit the trail with these, you'll...run out in a few minutes, actually, so perhaps bring some gorp as well.

8½ graham crackers
4 tablespoons cold unsalted butter
3 tablespoons granulated sugar

1 (14-ounce) can sweetened condensed milk
4 ounces unsweetened chocolate, chopped
30 large marshmallows, halved crosswise

1. Preheat oven to 350°F. Line a rimmed baking sheet with aluminum foil, extending foil over rim by 2". Spray foil with nonstick cooking spray.

2. Arrange crackers across bottom of prepared pan, breaking them as necessary to fit flush. Set aside.

3. In a small saucepan, combine butter and sugar and cook over low heat, stirring until butter is fully melted, about 3 minutes.

4. Drizzle butter mixture evenly over crackers, then spread out with a spatula until fully covered. Bake 8 minutes or until butter mixture is bubbling. Remove from heat and set aside.

5. In a medium microwave-safe bowl, combine milk and chocolate and microwave on high 1 minute. Stir until chocolate is melted and mixture is smooth. Pour chocolate mixture evenly over crackers and spread out with a clean spatula to fully cover.

6. Bake until chocolate mixture is set, about 6 minutes. Remove from oven and set aside.

7. Preheat oven to high broil.

8. Arrange marshmallow halves, cut-side down, over chocolate mixture, setting them about ½" apart. Broil about 7" from the heat source 30 seconds or until marshmallows are golden brown.

9. Remove from oven and cool in pan to room temperature, about 20 minutes, then refrigerate at least 1 hour, up to two days.

10. Lift bars from pan using foil as handle, place on a cutting board, and remove foil. Cut into twelve squares and serve.

A DISH BEST SERVED COLD?

It may sound sacrilegious or crazy, since s'mores are traditionally a food eaten as close to a fire as possible, but these are actually quite good chilled. If you have to make them in advance and store them before a game night, don't worry about sticking them in the refrigerator for a while and serving them chilled. One of the benefits of the chocolate being mixed with the condensed milk is that it'll retain a softer texture at any temperature, so they're just excellent right out of the icebox.

SHARDS OF ELEMENTAL CHAOS
Rainbow Candy Bark

Prep Time: 1 hour, 10 minutes | Cook Time: 10 minutes | Serves 8

In the vast infinity of the planar cosmos, the elements eternally swirl and clash against each other in a chaotic and endless explosion known as the Elemental Chaos. In this dimensional forge, all reality is created by the constant barrage of earth against fire, water against air, and so on, a dizzying and deadly ballet of cosmic creation. Obviously, some wizard eventually had the bright idea to head out there, crystallize a swathe of it all, and serve it up as a dessert. After a few dozen early adopters blew themselves up, we finally figured out how to do it. A sweet candy bark bursting with color and chaos, now available in your own kitchen, no Dimension Doors required.

1 pound white melting chocolate
2 ounces red melting chocolate
2 ounces orange melting chocolate
2 ounces yellow melting chocolate
2 ounces green melting chocolate

2 ounces blue melting chocolate
2 ounces purple melting chocolate
2 tablespoons rainbow sprinkles
1 (5-ounce) package Rainbow Nerds candy

1. Line a rimmed baking sheet with parchment paper.

2. Using separate small microwave-safe bowls, microwave melting chocolates one at a time on high in 20-second intervals until completely melted.

3. Spoon large dollops of white chocolate randomly on prepared pan, keeping most dollops near center of pan but still separated. Add dollops of colored chocolate across pan.

4. Lift and drop baking sheet onto a flat work surface from a 2"–3" height. Repeat until chocolate is spread out evenly over pan.

5. Using a knife tip, swirl chocolates. Immediately add sprinkles and Nerds candy evenly across swirled chocolate.

continued on next page

6. Cover and refrigerate chocolate at least 1 hour, up to 24 hours. When ready to serve, break into small, shard-like pieces and serve immediately.

COOLER EXPLOSIONS

Should you be interested in making this rainbow mayhem even cooler, there's no need to put on sunglasses and walk away from it without looking back. Just add 1 teaspoon of peppermint extract to the white melting chocolate, and divide an additional teaspoon as evenly as you can among the other colors. You'll probably also wish to omit the Nerds, but they're easily replaced with crushed candy cane to further boost the coolness. Who knew the timeless kiln at the center of all things could be so refreshing?

HALFLING HILLS
Roasted Brussels Sprouts

Prep Time: 10 minutes | Cook Time: 25 minutes | Serves 6

Traditional halflings like to keep things simple. Good food, good ale, and well-maintained farms with the farmhouse a humble but comfortable hole in the rolling hills of the country-side. They also can't get enough of cabbages, and while cabbage isn't the game plan here, another member of the *Brassica* family certainly is. These Brussels sprouts are everything that halflings love. Homey (literally, they look like halfling homes), roasty, and draped with unctuous bacon just keeping everything cozy and warm.

1½ pounds trimmed Brussels sprouts, cleaned
2 tablespoons olive oil

1 teaspoon salt
1 teaspoon ground black pepper
6 strips thick-cut bacon, cut into 1" pieces

1. Preheat oven to 400°F.

2. In a large bowl, add Brussels sprouts and drizzle with oil. Toss to coat.

3. Spread Brussels sprouts in a single, even layer on a large baking sheet. Sprinkle with salt and pepper. Sprinkle bacon evenly over Brussels sprouts.

4. Roast 25 minutes or until golden and lightly caramelized, turning halfway through cooking time. Serve immediately.

CHANGE KEEPS SPROUTING UP

Okay, fine. We're already hearing the pencils sharpening for missives telling us that modern halflings aren't tubby little homebodies anymore, and instead are dashing, tiny adventurers who seek out the thrill of battle, discovery, and treasure. For those so inclined, we offer this olive branch: Just say they aren't shaped like halfling houses; they're shaped like sling stones. Halflings still like slinging, right? Don't take that away from us too!

DUNGEON BARS
Chocolate-Dipped Pretzel Sticks

Prep Time: 45 minutes | Cook Time: 3 minutes | Serves 8

Dungeons, generally hewn rough from natural stone and either carved directly into the walls of a cave or stacked in cyclopean manner, still have creepy features throughout. Secret doors, deadly traps, and, of course, big-barred gates and prison walls so that the strong party members can feel cool about all the escaping they get to do. We've created this incredibly simple recipe for chocolate-dipped, topping-rolled pretzel sticks for the satisfaction of snapping them like so many doors in the way. Of course you can eat these, too, which is a huge bonus.

2 (10-ounce) bags semisweet chocolate chips
1 (12-ounce) bag pretzel logs
 (medium-sized sticks)

⅓ cup chopped nuts, any kind
2 tablespoons chocolate sprinkles
2 tablespoons shredded coconut

1. Line a rimmed baking sheet with wax paper.

2. Place chocolate chips in a double boiler over medium heat and stir continuously until fully melted, about 3 minutes.

3. Once chocolate is melted, quickly dip ⅔ of each pretzel in chocolate, turning to allow excess chocolate to drip back into double boiler.

4. Place dipped pretzels on prepared baking sheet and quickly spread nuts, sprinkles, and coconut over pretzels, mixing toppings between sticks or keeping toppings separate as desired.

5. Refrigerate 1 hour, then transfer sticks, standing on end, to a large jar or glass, and serve immediately.

BUT IT WAS BEND BARS!

Yes, fair enough, the original terminology used for getting past metal portcullises and the like was "Bend Bars/Lift Gates." Upon kitchen testing, bendable pretzels proved gummy and unappetizing, and some sacrifices were made on the altar of palatability.

THE LAVA PIT
Strawberry Jalapeño Chutney

Prep Time: 15 minutes | Cook Time: 35 minutes | Serves 8

Players love it when the DM sets battles on a big lava plain where there's pits of molten rock all over, as any player wants nothing so much as to shove villains to their doom without having to actually deplete their own hit points. Our chutney works a little differently: It's still a bubbling cauldron of red heat, but it won't deplete HP (if anything, it's so piquant and delicious, it might recover them), and you don't want to shove your enemies in there, just dip vegetables and breads.

1 large red onion, peeled and chopped

2 large jalapeños, seeded and minced

2 tablespoons water

3 cups diced fresh strawberries

2 cloves garlic, peeled and minced

2 tablespoons white vinegar

2 tablespoons maple syrup

½ teaspoon ground ginger

½ teaspoon ground coriander

1½ teaspoons brown mustard seeds

Juice of 1 medium lime

½ teaspoon salt

½ teaspoon ground black pepper

1. In a medium saucepan, sauté onion, jalapeños, and water 4–5 minutes over medium-low heat until onion starts to turn translucent, stirring continuously.

2. Add strawberries, garlic, vinegar, maple syrup, and spices. Increase heat to medium, and bring to a boil. Reduce heat to a low simmer, cover, and simmer 25–30 minutes until thick, stirring occasionally.

3. Remove from heat and stir in lime juice. Add salt and pepper. Serve immediately or chilled.

SACRIFICES TO THE PIT

Feeling concerned that the fire lords of the elemental planes have it in for you? Happy to help—just throw a few sacrifices into the lava and wait for the blessings to roll in. This is excellent on naan or paratha, spread over bread, and with just about anything dipped in it. That said, it's not molten stone, so you'll have to destroy anything dipped in it yourself. That's why we made it taste good!

ABYSSAL ENCOUNTER
Dilled Shrimp

Prep Time: 8 hours | Cook Time: 6 minutes | Serves 8

Strap on your arcanic breathing apparati and cast your water-breathing magics—it's time to descend to the lightless depths and fight all those cool aquatic monsters you keep hoping the DM will finally use. Weird, pallid, deadly things with uncountable arms, deadly claws, and glowing traps...and almost every single one of them is delicious with dill and white wine! Try these savory cold shrimp as an appetizer, and tell your friends they're fiendish dire amphipods.

2 quarts water
¼ cup coarse salt
⅓ cup granulated sugar
5 sprigs fresh dill
2 pounds medium shrimp, with shells

2 tablespoons vegetable oil
1 tablespoon white wine vinegar
1 tablespoon minced fresh dill
¼ teaspoon salt
¼ teaspoon ground black pepper

1. In a large pot, bring water to a boil over high heat. Once boiling, add salt, sugar, and dill sprigs, stirring continuously until sugar has dissolved, 2 minutes.

2. Add shrimp and cook until shells turn pink and meat is no longer translucent, about 4 minutes, then remove from heat.

3. Strain shrimp, discard dill sprigs, and transfer shrimp to a large bowl. Cover and refrigerate 30 minutes.

4. Peel and devein shrimp, discarding shells. Return shrimp to bowl and set aside.

5. In a small bowl, whisk together oil, vinegar, minced dill, salt, and pepper. Add to shrimp and toss to coat. Cover and refrigerate overnight. Serve cold.

AN ACID ATTACK

These deep-water morsels pair well with something acidic to bring their inherently murderous nature to the forefront. A cold cocktail sauce or even a spritz of lemon juice will liven them up considerably. And don't forget, deep-sea predators are ambush predators. Serve them up with a few full sprigs of fresh dill to give them a little kelp to hide behind.

SNOW-CAPPED HILLS
Watermelon Feta Skewers

Prep Time: 20 minutes | Cook Time: N/A | Serves 6

Arctic encounters often pit the party against colossal, shaggy beasts of the ice and snow. Yeti, mammoths, tigers, and the like abound, but there's already plenty of danger to be had in the terrain itself. Between ice chasms, subzero temperatures, and chilling winds, a trip to the snowy peaks of monster-infested mountains can be stressful. So skip all that and just enjoy a refreshing snack of fresh watermelon, salty feta cheese, and cooling mint. You'll find these as easy to assemble as they are to devour, and you'll wonder why you ever thought fighting a white dragon in a blizzard was a good idea.

1 medium seedless watermelon, cut into 1" cubes
1 (10.5-ounce) package feta cubes in brine
24 miniature mint leaves
1 tablespoon Italian seasoning
3 tablespoons balsamic glaze

1. Skewer one piece each watermelon, feta, and mint together on miniature skewers or large toothpicks, with watermelon at the base and mint on top.

2. Sprinkle feta with Italian seasoning, then drizzle skewers with balsamic glaze. Serve immediately.

FAVORED TERRAIN

Watermelon is a convenient (and delicious) base for this recipe because it's large enough to cut into attractive squares next to the feta, but it's hardly the only fruit that pairs well with your snow-block cheese of choice. Try substituting any melon, peaches, or even whole strawberries, and you'll see the flavor profile change instantly and in delightful ways.

FLAMES OF TARTARUS
Chorizo Chili

Prep Time: 30 minutes | Cook Time: 35 minutes | Serves 8

Deep in the fiery pits of the underworld, bubbling cauldrons of doom and lava are so common the local denizens barely even notice them anymore. (They honestly never did; the planes are infinite, and they're pretty busy with blood wars and torturing mortals anyway.) But up here, a good cauldron of lava and doom is a rare and celebrated affair. We've amped up this chili with chorizo, which brings a paprika and garlic heat to the party before you've even added the chili seasoning, which you will be making yourself. (Or not—you can replace the first seven ingredients with one of those packets from a grocery store. Live your own life!) This particular chili is also loaded with vegetables, hidden deep down in the sauce, because we authors have kids we need to trick into eating anything besides extruded corn foam products and chicken nuggets.

1 tablespoon chili powder
1 teaspoon ground cumin
¼ teaspoon cayenne pepper
¼ teaspoon garlic powder
½ teaspoon onion powder
1 teaspoon salt
½ teaspoon ground black pepper
1 medium carrot, roughly chopped
1 medium yellow squash, roughly chopped
1 medium green squash, roughly chopped
1 large white onion, peeled and chopped
1 large green bell pepper, seeded and chopped
2 teaspoons vegetable oil
1 pound ground beef
1 pound ground Mexican-style chorizo

1 (16-ounce) can black beans, drained and rinsed
1 (10-ounce) can chopped tomatoes and green chilies
1 large jalapeño, seeded and chopped
4 cups chicken or beef broth
2 tablespoons cornstarch
¼ cup tepid water
¼ medium red onion, peeled and chopped
1 bundle (about ¾ cup) fresh cilantro, chopped
1 (4-ounce) package tortilla strips
1 cup shredded sharp Cheddar cheese
1 (8-ounce) container sour cream

1. In a small bowl, combine chili powder, cumin, cayenne, garlic powder, onion powder, salt, and pepper. Set aside.

2. In a food processor, blitz carrot and both squashes until finely slivered. Drain any liquid and set aside.

3. In a large saucepan, cook white onion and bell pepper in oil over medium heat until onion begins to appear translucent, about 2–3 minutes.

4. Add beef and chorizo and cook, breaking apart and stirring, until fully browned, about 7 minutes. Remove from heat and use a slotted spoon or spatula to transfer to a large stockpot, reserving leftover oil.

5. Cook carrot and squash in saucepan used for meat over medium heat until fragrant and slightly browned, about 5 minutes. Remove from heat and transfer to stockpot.

6. Add beans, tomatoes and chilies mixture, and jalapeño to stockpot. Add broth until all ingredients are fully covered, place over medium heat, and bring to a simmer, about 10 minutes.

7. While the chili simmers, in a small bowl, combine cornstarch with water, mixing until no lumps remain. Add cornstarch slurry to chili and simmer 10 minutes.

8. Remove chili from heat and allow to cool 10 minutes. Serve with red onion, cilantro, tortilla strips, cheese, and sour cream on the side for topping.

BLOOD IS THICKER THAN CHILI (NO, IT ISN'T, NOT IF YOU MADE IT RIGHT)

We mentioned blood wars earlier, and you might be wondering how that fits into a chili-based metaphor. It's easy enough to explain: The denizens of the Abyss and Tartarus war forever over whether chili with beans in it counts as chili. Personally, we say yes. We're not demons or devils, and chili is just a big spicy pot of mostly meat and sauce. Call us Chaotic Neutral if you must, but we're fine with it. Chili tastes just as good in Limbo.

Let's get meta! This chapter will deal with the trappings of gameplay itself, providing a range of recipes that highlight the shared universal tools and in-jokes that unite RPG players even as their characters remain unique. These recipes are the ties that bind! Whether it's a DM's pizza you're finally allowed to touch or an edible cookie hex map, you're certain to find that everything in this chapter…rules. It's all rules.

THE DM'S PIZZA
Next-Day Pizza Dough

Prep Time: 9 hours | Cook Time: 12 minutes | Makes enough for 3 (12") thin-crust pizzas

"Don't touch it!" warns the first page of so many RPG books, informing us all that the DM, though we might have considered them a friend and fellow player up until this moment, is actually a dangerous predator, willing to kill you before sharing any food. That's why our recipe includes enough dough to make three pizzeria-style thin-crust pizzas, crisp and delightful, as our research has displayed that even the most rigorous of DMs can only defend two pizzas at once.

1½ cups warm (110°F) water
1 tablespoon granulated sugar
1 tablespoon olive oil
¾ teaspoon active dry yeast

4½ cups all-purpose flour, divided
1 teaspoon salt
Toppings of choice (pepperoni, sliced
   tomatoes, spinach)

1. In a small bowl, combine water, sugar, oil, and yeast. Set aside 3 minutes to allow yeast to foam and bloom.

2. In a large bowl or stand mixer fitted with a dough hook attachment, sift 4 cups flour and salt. Add yeast mixture and stir.

3. If kneading by hand, transfer dough to a floured work surface and knead 3 minutes. If using dough hook in a stand mixer, knead on medium speed 2 minutes.

4. Once dough is soft and shiny but still slightly sticky, begin pinching edges and folding under in a circular motion to shape dough into a ball. Place dough in a large oiled bowl seam-side down. Coat dough surface with oil to prevent drying, and cover bowl with plastic wrap. Refrigerate at least overnight, up to 24 hours. Dough will keep for up to two weeks.

5. Remove dough from refrigerator at least 2 hours before cooking. Transfer from bowl to a well-floured work surface and punch out air. Reshape into a ball, then roll into a small log.

continued on next page

6. Divide log into three equal portions and allow to rest 10 minutes. When ready to cook, roll one dough ball out to a thin circle approximately 12" in diameter on a floured pan or pizza steel. Spread toppings of choice over dough and bake at 475°F 10–12 minutes or until cheese is melted and beginning to brown and crust is beginning to char. Repeat with remaining two dough balls. Serve hot.

PIZZA THAT CAN BE TOPPED

Perhaps the greatest aspect to these ready-made doughs is that you can turn pizza craft into another party activity for the night. Have sauce and cheese ready, and bowls full of your favorite (and we suppose everyone else's, too) toppings out, and make it a pizza party from start to finish. Pepperoni, onions, mushrooms, whatever you like. We are particularly partial to pickled peppers and crisp bacon.

INSPIRATION POINTS
Roasted Garlic

Prep Time: 15 minutes | Cook Time: 1 hour | Serves 4

This is one of the simplest recipes you'll find, and yet it's one that's incredibly rewarding. These cloves of garlic are slow-roasted in olive oil and steamed until they're so tender you can spread them on bread with your thumb. Just eating one is a complex and invigorating experience, rewarding in both allium sharpness and roasty sweetness, and it makes a great marking point to when you hit an in-game milestone. Toss one to a player when they crack a puzzle or finish a challenge, and they'll remember it. They'll also have some garlic breath, so have some Inspiration Mints around too.

*2 large bulbs garlic,
 separated and peeled*

*1 tablespoon olive oil
2 tablespoons water*

1. Preheat oven to 350°F.

2. Place garlic cloves on a sheet of aluminum foil large enough to wrap around garlic completely. Fold edges of foil up to catch liquid.

3. Drizzle oil over cloves, add water, and seal foil. Bake 1 hour or until garlic is completely soft. Remove from foil and serve.

A POINTED SUGGESTION

While there's certainly nothing wrong with tossing a few cloves of roasted garlic directly into your mouth, they are exceptional when served with something crunchy to add texture. Rosemary crackers and crusty French bread are both perfect options that will take these from experience points to victory incarnate.

ADVENTURE MODULES
Monkey Bread Variations

Prep Time: 10 minutes | Cook Time: 43 minutes | Serves 6

When you lack the time to craft a complicated adventure, you're in luck, because adventure modules do most of the hard work for you. They'll be the first to tell you where the secret doors are and how many orcs are in the armory. They're fantastic because they allow you to be flexible and look like the hero, and the same is true of these rolls. Easy to throw together and modify, these modules will save you at game night after game night.

1 tablespoon ground cinnamon
1 cup granulated sugar
3 (16.3-ounce) cans refrigerated biscuits
(like Pillsbury Grands!)

½ cup cold unsalted butter
1 cup packed light brown sugar

1. Preheat oven to 350°F. Liberally coat a Bundt pan with nonstick cooking spray.

2. In a small bowl, combine cinnamon and granulated sugar.

3. Separate biscuits and cut each into quarters. Roll each biscuit quarter in cinnamon sugar mixture until well coated on all sides, then place in Bundt pan in a single layer, filling up the bottom of the pan.

4. In a small saucepan, combine butter and brown sugar and bring to a boil over medium heat. Stir well until all sugar is dissolved, about 3 minutes, then remove from heat and pour over biscuit quarters.

5. Bake 35–40 minutes until golden brown. Serve warm.

MODULE A4: SCOURGE OF THE GARLIC BUTTER

For savory modules, simply omit the cinnamon and both sugars. When you're crafting your rolling mix, make it from 1½ teaspoons garlic powder, 3 tablespoons dried parsley, 3 tablespoons chopped green onion, and ¼ teaspoon salt. Roll your dough balls in that mixture, then once they're in the pan, generously cover with Parmesan cheese and about 5 tablespoons butter before baking as directed. Serve with warm marinara, and you've got a savory module, ready to rumble.

THE MONTY HAUL
Peanut Butter Custard Blast

Prep Time: 2 hours, 45 minutes | Cook Time: 12 minutes | Serves 8

A term that refers to the man himself, Monty Hall, longtime host of the TV show *Let's Make a Deal*, the Monty Haul in RPG terminology is a campaign that is simply dripping with treasure, magical equipment, and loot as far as the eye can see. Since there aren't many recipes for +3 swords, we've opted to craft our own decadent offering, a rich pie filled with homemade peanut butter custard, with a cookie crust, and topped with crumbled nuts and chocolate that'll leave you feeling as rich as any dragon's hoard.

For Crust
2 cups Oreo cookie crumbs
2 tablespoons granulated sugar
⅓ cup melted unsalted butter
For Filling
1½ cups granulated sugar
⅓ cup cornstarch
2 tablespoons all-purpose flour
½ teaspoon salt

6 cups whole milk
6 large egg yolks, beaten
1 cup creamy peanut butter
For Topping
2 cups heavy whipping cream
1 tablespoon confectioners' sugar
6 peanut butter cups, chopped
½ cup chopped salted peanuts
2 tablespoons chocolate syrup

1. Preheat oven to 375°F.

2. To make Crust: In a medium bowl, combine cookie crumbs and granulated sugar. Stir in butter.

3. Press Crust onto bottom of a greased 13" × 9" baking dish. Bake 8 minutes or until set. Remove from oven and cool on a wire rack, about 10 minutes.

4. To make Filling: In a large saucepan, combine granulated sugar, cornstarch, flour, and salt. Stir in milk until smooth and consistent. Cook over medium-high heat until thickened and bubbling, then reduce heat to low and stir 2 minutes. Remove from heat.

5. In a small bowl, add egg yolks and stir in a small amount of hot sugar mixture to temper eggs. Stir and mix thoroughly before pouring egg

mixture into saucepan with remaining sugar mixture and stirring to mix. Place back on the stove over medium heat and bring to a gentle boil, then cook, stirring continuously, 2 minutes.

6. Remove pan from heat. Stir in peanut butter until smooth, then pour Filling over Crust. Cool to room temperature, about 20 minutes, before covering and refrigerating at least 2 hours, up to overnight.

7. To make Topping: In a large bowl, beat cream until it begins to thicken. Add confectioners' sugar and continue to beat until stiff peaks form. Spread over Filling. Sprinkle with peanut butter cups and peanuts and drizzle with chocolate syrup. Serve chilled.

THE MONTY HAUL PROBLEM

Monty and the *Let's Make a Deal* show spawned more than just the term that players still use to describe RPG campaigns. It also led to a famously head-scratching probability puzzle. Should you switch doors after the goat is revealed? Yes, apparently you should. There isn't room here to go into the solutions to the Monty Hall problem; just google "Marilyn vos Savant + Monty Hall" and have your mind blown later. For you, right now, the Monty Haul problem is sharing. It's hard, but, yes, you generally have to.

HEX GRIDS
Hexagonal Sugar Cookies with Landscape Icing

—————•◆•◆•—————

Prep Time: 8 hours | Cook Time: 12 minutes | Yields 24 cookies

Ah, overland travel, last refuge of the hexagonal map. Old-school players will reminisce about the days of sandbox play, wandering from hex to hex, exploring dangers that could be far too intense for them, and checking off the grid as they go. Here you'll find an interesting alternative. An edible landscape hex. Instead of checking off the grid as you explore it, you get to eat your way through the countryside of forests, mountains, deserts, and more, all rendered in a delicious almond-infused sugar cookie painted with easy-to-make royal icing. Sandbox exploration never tasted so good.

For Cookies
1 cup room-temperature unsalted butter
1 ounce room-temperature cream cheese
1 cup granulated sugar
1 large egg
1 teaspoon vanilla extract
½ teaspoon almond extract
2¾ cups all-purpose flour
1½ teaspoons baking powder
1 teaspoon salt

For Icing
3 cups confectioners' sugar
4 tablespoons whole milk, divided
1½ tablespoons light corn syrup
½ teaspoon vanilla extract
3 drops each various gel food colorings

1. **To make Cookies:** In a large bowl, use an electric mixer to beat butter and cream cheese until well blended. Add granulated sugar and continue to beat until light and fluffy. Add egg, vanilla, and almond extract and continue to beat until combined.

2. In a small bowl, whisk together flour, baking powder, and salt.

3. Add ½ of flour mixture to butter mixture and beat on low until incorporated. Add remaining flour mixture and beat until a soft dough forms.

4. Gather dough into a ball and use a large knife or bench scraper to cut in half. Press each dough half into a large disc and cover tightly with plastic wrap. Refrigerate at least 8 hours, up to two days.

continued on next page

5. When ready to bake, remove one or both discs of cookie dough from refrigerator and let rest at room temperature.

6. Preheat oven to 350°F. Line two rimmed baking sheets with parchment paper.

7. Roll out dough on a clean, well-floured work surface to ¼" thick. Using a cookie cutter, cut dough into hexagons and place 2" apart on prepared baking sheets.

8. Bake 8–12 minutes until very lightly browned around edges and bottom. Remove from oven and cool on pan 4 minutes, then transfer cookies to a wire rack to cool completely, at least 30 minutes.

9. To make Icing: In a medium bowl, combine confectioners' sugar, 3 tablespoons milk, corn syrup, and vanilla. If icing is too thick to pipe, add remaining 1 tablespoon milk.

10. Divide icing mixture into separate small bowls and add food colorings to create desired colors. (Add 1–2 more drops of each color for deeper/brighter colors.)

11. Transfer icing to piping bags fitted with piping tips. Pipe icing onto cookies to create landscape elements, such as forests, oceans, and deserts.

12. Allow cookies to rest and icing to dry 3 hours before serving.

OLD-SCHOOL VERISIMILITUDE

If you're looking to take this admittedly high-concept cookie map up a notch, you certainly could. Check out the baking aisle at a grocery store or find a specialty store and get additional textural elements like tree sprinkles (easily found around the holidays), candy sharks, and crumbled vanilla wafer cookies for "sand" that will easily stick to the cookie while the icing is drying and take your cookies from awesome to a functional hex map.

IMPROVISED GRENADES
Cheese Bombs

Prep Time: 5 minutes | Cook Time: 10 minutes | Serves 4

Barbarians at the gates, and you don't have time to carefully craft "safe" grenades to hurl down there and stem the tide? Just grab handfuls of whatever's around and throw it instead. Similarly, here's a snack made from stuff you've probably just got around anyway, ready and hot on the table in 15 minutes, and as efficacious, cheesy, and delicious as anything you could cook in twice the time.

1 (16-ounce) can refrigerated biscuits
4 sticks mozzarella string cheese, cut
  horizontally into 1" chunks
4 tablespoons melted unsalted butter

1 teaspoon Italian seasoning
1 teaspoon garlic powder
½ teaspoon salt
2 tablespoons finely chopped flat-leaf parsley

1. Preheat oven to 400°F. Line a baking sheet with aluminum foil and grease with nonstick cooking spray.

2. Separate biscuits and place 1 cheese piece in center of each biscuit, wrapping dough around cheese and pinching to seal. Place each dough ball seam-side down on prepared baking sheet.

3. Bake biscuits 10 minutes or until lightly golden brown.

4. While biscuits bake, in a small bowl, combine butter, Italian seasoning, garlic powder, and salt.

5. Immediately drizzle or brush butter mixture over baked biscuits. Sprinkle with parsley and serve immediately.

PACKING IN EXPLOSIVE FLAVORS

These are already quite good on their own, but they can be upgraded from improvised to battle-ready with a few easy additions. Serve alongside a bowl of warm marinara for an easy and delicious dip, and if you want to amp up performance more, store-bought meatballs cooked according to package directions, halved, and placed in the center of each biscuit with the cheese turn your grenades into a full and explosively delicious meal.

SPOT CHECKS
Caprese "Eyes"

Prep Time: 20 minutes | Cook Time: N/A | Serves 4

Caprese is a classic Italian salad format that takes a few simple ingredients and highlights their flavors in perfect harmony. It's so easy that you can really stretch your creative muscles when playing with the format, which is why ours are shaped like terrifying staring eyes. We've named these after spot checks, the calls that DMs will make to have players attempt to notice hidden or obscure details about their environment using their spot or perception scores. We recommend giving players a bonus if they've eaten one recently. Keep your eyes open, and these eyes handy, because they're tasty!

12 green olives, sliced into rings

12 black olives, halved lengthwise

24 large fresh basil leaves

1 (11-ounce) package grape tomatoes, halved lengthwise

1 (8-ounce) package pearl mozzarella in brine, halved

¼ teaspoon salt

¼ teaspoon ground black pepper

1 tablespoon olive oil

1. Stuff each green olive ring with one black olive half, cutting black olives down to fit as required.

2. On a large serving tray, lay out basil leaves, place one tomato half on each, cut-side up, then layer one cheese half on top, and place an olive "pupil" onto cheese. Sprinkle with salt, pepper, and oil and serve immediately.

EYES OF THE EYE TYRANT

You're probably aware of that huge ball monster with the maw and the eyestalks that's found in just about every Monster Manual. But hey, did you know it's a highly protected legal IP? Well, now you do. Would these appetizers, connected by celery stalks to a "body" made of a bowl of dipping balsamic glaze, make a phenomenal table centerpiece? Of course they would. But we can't recommend that or tell you what to call it. That's okay, though, you know.

DIFFICULTY SPIKES
Chicken Satay Skewers with Peanut Sauce

Prep Time: 30 minutes | Cook Time: 6 minutes | Serves 4

Don't let the name fool you; despite being a reference to occasional bursts of unexpected trials and tribulations in an otherwise straightforward game session, these chicken skewers are in fact deceptively easy to make, and worth any trouble you may encounter along the way too. *Kecap manis*, an Indonesian sweet soy sauce that gives these skewers their sticky charm, can be difficult to source, but it will generally be available at Asian markets. Don't forget to pair them with the peanut sauce, which is so smooth and creamy it'll make any troubles at the table go down smooth.

For Skewers
3 medium shallots, roughly chopped
2 garlic cloves, peeled
1½ teaspoons crushed fresh or bottled ginger
2 long red chilies, roughly chopped
1 pound chicken tenderloins, cut into
 1" pieces
1 (8-ounce) container kecap manis
 (or sweet soy sauce)

For Peanut Sauce
¾ cup creamy peanut butter
¼ cup rice vinegar
⅓ cup tamari or soy sauce
3 tablespoons honey
1½ teaspoons crushed fresh or bottled ginger
2 cloves garlic, peeled and crushed
¼ teaspoon red pepper flakes
4 tablespoons unsweetened coconut milk
1 tablespoon chopped roasted peanuts

1. To make Skewers: In the bowl of a food processor, add shallots, garlic, ginger, and chilies and pulse until smooth.

2. In a medium bowl, toss chicken with shallot mixture and *kecap manis*. Cover bowl with plastic wrap and refrigerate 30 minutes.

3. Thread chicken pieces evenly onto skewers. In a large frying pan, cook skewers in batches over medium-high heat 3 minutes on each side until browned and cooked through. Remove from heat and transfer to a large plate. Cover with aluminum foil.

4. To make Peanut Sauce: In a medium bowl, combine all ingredients except coconut milk and peanuts, then add coconut milk while stirring until desired consistency (slightly thicker than ketchup) is reached.

5. Transfer to a serving bowl and sprinkle peanuts over top. Serve alongside Skewers.

FLATTENING THE CURVE

If a spike of difficulty seems a little extreme, you can ramp up to it by rounding out the meal with a few carefully curated sides. A little jasmine rice and a cucumber salad will cool the intensity down a bit and allow you to focus on the task at hand. Never get caught out in a tough situation again!

SHORT RESTS
Chorizo and Egg Tacos

Prep Time: 15 minutes | Cook Time: 13 minutes | Serves 6

When you've only got a little time to get some hit points back and your head in the game, you'll never be able to get two meals in. That's why we've got an entrée that captures the best aspects of breakfast and dinner—warm soft tacos bursting with scrambled egg and chorizo—so that you can fill up, get a few spells back (if you're a warlock), and steel yourself to hit the field again.

12 ounces Mexican-style chorizo sausage, casings removed

12 large eggs

½ teaspoon salt

¼ teaspoon ground black pepper

6 tablespoons whole milk

12 (5") corn tortillas

1 cup chopped hothouse tomatoes

1 large avocado, peeled, pitted, and chopped

4 tablespoons Cotija cheese

¼ cup chopped fresh cilantro leaves

1. In a large skillet, brown chorizo over medium heat, breaking it up as it cooks. When fully browned, about 7 minutes, transfer to a large, paper towel–lined bowl to drain.

2. In a medium bowl, whisk eggs with salt, pepper, and milk, then pour into the same skillet used for chorizo. Reduce heat to medium-low and cook, stirring gently and carefully scraping mixture from the sides of skillet to form curds, until slightly runny, about 3–4 minutes.

3. Add chorizo back into pan and stir to combine, about 2 minutes, then remove from heat.

4. Stack tortillas and wrap in a damp paper towel, then microwave on high 30 seconds. Leave wrapped until ready to assemble. (Alternatively, you can warm them over an open stove burner on medium-high heat, cooking 20–30 seconds per side.)

continued on next page

5. Assemble tacos, scooping an even amount of chorizo and egg mixture into each tortilla and topping with tomato, avocado, cheese, and cilantro. Serve warm.

LONG RESTS?

Sure, you could try to improve on these by separating them for a Long Rest, having a nice plate of scrambled eggs, memorizing a bunch of spells, and filling up on tacos before the dungeon calls, but the two combined are really good! Just have some for breakfast and the leftovers for lunch. That way, even if you get ambushed by your "nice" DM, you'll still have spares for at least a second Short Rest.

Appendix: Recipe Breakdown

While the recipes in this book can be enjoyed whenever you and your fellow adventurers desire, some are the perfect fit for a filling breakfast around the game table, while others prove to satisfy a sweet tooth during a late-night session.

DINNER

APPETIZERS AND SNACKS

US/Metric Conversion Chart

VOLUME CONVERSIONS

US VOLUME MEASURE	METRIC EQUIVALENT
⅛ teaspoon	0.5 milliliter
¼ teaspoon	1 milliliter
½ teaspoon	2 milliliters
1 teaspoon	5 milliliters
½ tablespoon	7 milliliters
1 tablespoon (3 teaspoons)	15 milliliters
2 tablespoons (1 fluid ounce)	30 milliliters
¼ cup (4 tablespoons)	60 milliliters
⅓ cup	90 milliliters
½ cup (4 fluid ounces)	125 milliliters
⅔ cup	160 milliliters
¾ cup (6 fluid ounces)	180 milliliters
1 cup (16 tablespoons)	250 milliliters
1 pint (2 cups)	500 milliliters
1 quart (4 cups)	1 liter (about)

OVEN TEMPERATURE CONVERSIONS

DEGREES FAHRENHEIT	DEGREES CELSIUS
200 degrees F	95 degrees C
250 degrees F	120 degrees C
275 degrees F	135 degrees C
300 degrees F	150 degrees C
325 degrees F	160 degrees C
350 degrees F	180 degrees C
375 degrees F	190 degrees C
400 degrees F	205 degrees C
425 degrees F	220 degrees C
450 degrees F	230 degrees C

BAKING PAN SIZES

AMERICAN	METRIC
8 × 1½ inch round baking pan	20 × 4 cm cake tin
9 × 1½ inch round baking pan	23 × 3.5 cm cake tin
11 × 7 × 1½ inch baking pan	28 × 18 × 4 cm baking tin
13 × 9 × 2 inch baking pan	30 × 20 × 5 cm baking tin
2 quart rectangular baking dish	30 × 20 × 3 cm baking tin
15 × 10 × 2 inch baking pan	30 × 25 × 2 cm baking tin (Swiss roll tin)
9 inch pie plate	22 × 4 or 23 × 4 cm pie plate
7 or 8 inch springform pan	18 or 20 cm springform or loose bottom cake tin
9 × 5 × 3 inch loaf pan	23 × 13 × 7 cm or 2 lb narrow loaf or pâté tin
1½ quart casserole	1.5 liter casserole
2 quart casserole	2 liter casserole

Index

About the Authors

Jef Aldrich is a professional podcaster from San Diego. Along with Jon Taylor, he has been building a podcast brand outside of the big network channels. Jef started entertaining people as a Sea World tour guide and eventually just started being funny for a living on his own. Jef is the coauthor of *Düngeonmeister*. He is also a cocreator and cohost of the *System Mastery* podcast with Jon, in which they review and comment on odd classic RPGs, poking fun at obscure stories and systems while taking games for a spin.

Jon Taylor is also a professional podcaster from San Diego. He has a degree in English literature from the University of California, Santa Cruz. He spent several years as a stand-up comic on the East Coast before moving back to Southern California. Jon is the coauthor of *Düngeonmeister*. Jon is also a cocreator and cohost of the *System Mastery* podcast with Jef Aldrich, in which they review and comment on odd classic RPGs, poking fun at obscure stories and systems while taking games for a spin.

Cocktail recipes your whole gaming group will love!

Pick up or download your copy today!